WORK, LIFE, AND FAMILY IMBALANCE

WORK, LIFE, AND FAMILY IMBALANCE

How to Level the Playing Field

Edited by

Michele A. Paludi and
Presha E. Neidermeyer

Westport, Connecticut
London

Library of Congress Cataloging-in-Publication Data

Work, life, and family imbalance : how to level the playing field / edited by Michele A. Paludi
and Presha E. Neidermeyer.
    p. cm.
    Includes bibliographical references and index.
    ISBN 978–0–275–99390–0 (alk. paper)
1. Work and family—United States. 2. Working mothers—United States. 3. Sex
discrimination against women—United States. 4. Personnel management—United States.
5. Family policy—United States. I. Paludi, Michele Antoinette. II. Neidermeyer, Presha E.
    HD4904.25.W7365 2007
    306.3′6—dc22   2007022981

British Library Cataloguing in Publication Data is available.

Library of Congress Catalog Card Number: 2007022981
ISBN-13: 978–0–275–99390–0

First published in 2007

Praeger Publishers, 88 Post Road West, Westport, CT 06881
An imprint of Greenwood Publishing Group, Inc.
www.praeger.com

Printed in the United States of America

The paper used in this book complies with the
Permanent Paper Standard issued by the National
Information Standards Organization (Z39.48–1984).

10 9 8 7 6 5 4 3 2 1

For Antoinette and Michael Paludi:
For integrating work and family lives on behalf of Rosalie,
Lucille, and myself.

—Michele A. Paludi

******

For Eliza Grace and Jack August:
May you learn today's lessons early and help to solve the new
problems when they arise.

—Presha E. Neidermeyer

Contents

Preface

Janet Sigal

Work/life balance is related to gender equality worldwide and gender roles. If women are discriminated against by being prevented from engaging in paid work outside the home, are placed in subordinate roles in the workplace, or are paid less for comparable jobs than men, then this inequality will negatively impact the family and role modeling for girl children in the family. If the traditional gender roles (i.e., males as the breadwinners and women as child caregivers) are institutionalized in the culture, these roles will reinforce the subordinate position of women in the workplace. In addition, if adequate child care is not provided by the government or the private sector, this lack will negatively impact women in the workplace.

As indicated in a pamphlet by UNICEF, "The State of the World's Children 2007: Executive Summary," "While there has been great progress in recent decades in engaging women in the labour force, there has been considerably less advance on improving the conditions under which they work, recognizing their unpaid work, eliminating discriminatory practices and laws related to property and inheritance rights, and providing support for childcare. Ensuring that women and men have equal opportunities to generate and manage income is an important step towards realizing women's rights" (p. 37).

Also in the pamphlet, it is indicated that unpaid work in the house in many countries constitutes the major part of the work of women and even if they do work, they are still much more responsible for housework and child care. The example of Mexico is given: Despite working, women's participation in work in the house is, on the average, thirty-three hours per week compared with men's six hours per week. The UNICEF pamphlet also suggests that less pay for women than men may result in even 20 percent less pay in some countries. "Women are also more likely to work in more precarious forms of employment with low earnings, little financial security and few or no social benefits" (p. 10). The suggestion is that governments should undertake legislative, financial, and administrative measures to create a strong and enabling environment for women's entrepreneurship and participation in the labor market. Social policies should be promoted to tackle discrimination in the workplace and to enable women and men to reconcile their work and family responsibilities" (p. 10).

At the UN Commission on Social Development (February 2007), Mr. Juan Somavia, Director General of the International Labour Office (ILO), stated "policy recommendations to increase the number of women workers worldwide":

1. Allow flexible working time, job sharing and teamwork;
2. Part-time working should be included in pension systems and these workers should not be forced to retire early;
3. Employers should be convinced that it is in their interest to hire and keep women —especially older women—in their jobs;
4. Governments should produce incentives to employers to hire and keep women workers and provide appropriate training. (Gastaldo, 2007)

An article by S. Lerner in the *New York Times Magazine* (2007) suggested that the low birthrate in "advanced countries" can be explained partly by the barriers faced by women who want to work. If the woman has to choose between motherhood and a career, because she will be penalized financially and professionally, she may choose the career and not risk losing her position if she decides to opt out of the work setting to raise her children. Lerner suggested that higher birthrates in Europe are associated with better government support and requirements of "pay parity and benefits...females being offered more flexibility in part-time work...and extensive public child-care" programs (p. 20). Lerner also related the issue to traditional gender-role nations, where child care is relegated to individuals to solve. Although these data are only correlational, it was interesting that this conclusion goes against traditional thought that working women would be less likely to have children than nonworking women.

Gastaldo (2007), in a presentation to the NGO on Ageing at the UN, suggested that the retirement phase continues the unfair situation for women. Since women have more breaks in employment due to child rearing, and often are employed on a part-time basis, and even if employed full-time, often earn less than men, they have less access to decent pension plans, which require a significant amount of work credit before individuals may access pension plans.

A study by Heymann, Earle, & Hanchate (2004) reviewed the increases in the participation of women in the workforce. It has increased "from 26 to 38% in the Caribbean, from 16 to 33% in Central America, from 17 to 25% in the Middle East, from 23 to 31% in North Africa, from 31 to 46% in North America, from 27 to 43% in Oceana, from 31 to 41% in Western Europe, and from 21 to 35% in South America since 1960 (ILO, 1999; World Bank Group, 2000)" (p. 248). The authors suggested that women constitute "at least one third of the labour force...except in the Middle East and North Africa" (p. 248). The authors examined workers who spend over sixty hours during the week working, and possibly seventy hours if commuting is included in the statistics, including workers in Brazil, Mexico, South Africa, and Vietnam. They concluded that often individuals who work long hours are those who cannot afford child care, in particular, single-parent families. When unpaid work was included, women were more likely to work longer hours than men, which, as the authors concluded, could negatively affect their "health and well-being." In addition, if child care is not accessible (e.g., if the parents cannot afford child care), then the children either are alone or are subjected to inferior and negligent child care, which can affect their well-being and their upbringing.

Lewis and Smithson (2001) conducted a prospective study of individuals' expectations concerning the state or employer's provision of support for families. In a study of younger individuals who have not really experienced the workplace yet, focus groups of participants from Norway, Sweden, Portugal, Ireland, and the United Kingdom were conducted. The authors determined that "participants in Sweden and Norway, where welfare states are based on an equality contract, demonstrated a higher sense of entitlement to support from the state and for employer flexibility in terms of working hours. Conversely, most participants in Ireland, Portugal, and the UK expected less from both the state and the employer" (pp. 1474–1475). The authors stated that "gender appears to be particularly significant in influencing what is perceived as normative, appropriate and feasible....Hence women with traditional gender expectations will feel less entitled to support to enable them to work when they have family responsibilities, and men less entitled to employer support for involvement in caring" (p. 1458).

Therefore, both traditional gender roles versus nontraditional gender roles influence whether or not women face barriers to employment and negative aspects of work, including a lack of support for child care.

Another aspect is individualism-collectivism. Spector, et al. (2004) indicated that in individualist societies, workers would experience more work/family stress if they experience demands from both arenas (i.e., see both areas as competing), whereas in collectivist societies, work is seen as "a means of supporting the family" (p. 124). Individuals in collectivist countries would not see the two areas as competing, and, therefore, longer work hours would not be associated with increased stress. The authors found that "Anglos... demonstrate a stronger positive relation between work hours and work-family stressors than Chinese and Latins" (p. 120). The Anglo sample consisted of Australia, Canada, England, New Zealand, and the United States. The Chinese/Latin America sample consisted of China: Hong Kong, People's Republic, and Taiwan; Latin America: Argentina, Brazil, Colombia, Ecuador, Mexico, Peru, and Uruguay.

In light of the fact that in so many countries around the world, women are entering the workforce in larger numbers, and yet working conditions for women have not improved to a significant degree, this book should add considerably to the literature on work/family stressors and the means of achieving a good balance between work and family obligations. If women are to derive significant satisfaction from the work experience, and also be able to demand more flexibility to enable them to fulfill family responsibilities, it is important to examine barriers and positive forces that affect this balance. This book represents an impressive attempt to examine the relevant issues in an objective, thorough, and empirical manner.

References

Gastaldo, E. (2007, February). Employment and decent work for all. A statement prepared by E. Gastaldo of the ILO Office for the United Nations and presented at the NGO Committee on Ageing in New York.

Heymann, J., Earle, A., & Hanchate, A. (2004). Bringing a global perspective to community work and family: An examination of extended work hours in families in four countries. *Community, Work and Family*, 7, 247–272.

Lerner, S. (2007). The motherhood experiment. In the *New York Times Magazine*, 3/4/07, p. 20.

Lewis, S., & Smithson, J. (2001). Sense of entitlement to support for the reconciliation of employment and family life. *Human Relations*, 54, 1455–1481.

Spector, P., Cooper, C., Poelmans, S., Allen, T., O'Driscoll, M., Sanchez, J., Siu, O., Dewe, P., Hart, P., & Lu, L. (2004). A cross-national comparative study of work-family stressors, working hours, and well-being: China and Latin America versus the Anglo World. *Personnel Psychology*, 57, 119–142.

UNICEF (2006, December). The state of the world's children 2007: Executive Summary. Published by the United Nations Children's Fund.

Acknowledgments ❧

We thank Nick Philipson and Jeff Olson for their support, encouragement, and sage advice regarding this book. They helped make this book become a reality. We have enjoyed working with both Nick and Jeff, as well as other members of the Praeger family. We also acknowledge Greenwood Publishing Group, Inc.'s permission to reprint Julie Magid's chapter on pregnancy discrimination.

We also thank the contributors and are honored to have your work in this volume. Your dedication to quality-of-life issues and making employers more sensitive to the needs of their employees is inspiring.

Michele Paludi also thanks students in her winter and spring term, 2007 courses on human resource management and educational psychology for their comments on earlier drafts of this book. It has been exhilarating to see a new generation continuing to work toward feminist principles.

Michele also extends her sincere thanks to the following individuals who listened and offered advice and comfort during the lonely times of writing: Rosalie Paludi, Lucille Paludi, Carmen Paludi, Jr., Presha Neidermeyer, and Paula Lundberg-Love.

Presha appreciates the support of AA and Ellen Neidermeyer, Mandy Noelle, Jay, Don, and Tracy in this as in all things. You make the life part more enjoyable—thank you. She also gratefully acknowledges the guidance of her friend and colleague, Michele Paludi, with this book.

Introduction

Michele A. Paludi and Presha E. Neidermeyer

I can't have a baby. I have a 12 o'clock lunch meeting.
—J.C. Wiatt in *Baby Boom*

These famous words, uttered by J.C. Wiatt (portrayed by Diane Keaton) in *Baby Boom*, sum up the sentiment of most employed women who try to integrate family and work life—roles that at most times appear to be incompatible. Rosabeth Moss Kanter's book *Work and Family in the United States: A Critical Review and Agenda for Research and Policy* (1977) brought the issue of work/life balance to the forefront of organizations. The incompatibility between work and family roles is reflected in the following research findings (Brooks-Gunn, Han, & Waldfogel, 2002; Gurchiek, 2007; Heymann, 2000; Peeters, et al., 2005; Strassel, et al., 2006):

- Women carry more of the workload at home;
- Employed women do substantially more caregiving to children and elder parents;
- Employed women are more likely to lack basic fringe benefits needed to care for their family;
- Employed women are more likely to lack job flexibility;
- Salary inequities still exist, especially for women of color;
- While each day more than 350,000 children of employed parents are ill, very few child care centers have provisions for sick children so parents can go to work.

Ivy Baker Priest noted, with respect to this incompatibility,

Any woman who has a career and a family automatically develops something in the way of two personalities, like two sides of a dollar bill, each different in design ....Her problem is to keep one from draining the life from the other.

Unfortunately, this incompatibility between being a mother and being employed has been made popular due to psychologists' insistence on mothers remaining at home to ensure the children's optimal development (Clark-Stewart, 1993). According to Russo (1979), a motherhood mandate exists: the belief that the primary career roles of women center around domestic and child-care responsibilities:

Characterizing motherhood as prescribed, however, does not adequately communicate the centrality of this behavior to the definition of the adult female. "Being pretty" is also prescribed, but one can compensate for not being pretty (by being a "good mother"), for example. It is a woman's raison d'etre. It is mandatory. The mandate requires that one have at least two children (historically as many as possible and preferably sons) and that one raises them "well." As long as this situation exists for the vast majority of women in Western society and the world in general, prohibitions may be eliminated and options widened, but change will occur only insofar as women are first able to fulfill their mandate of motherhood. (p. 144)

The reality, however, is that the majority of women with children are employed and work outside of their home (Brooks-Gunn, Han, & Waldfogel, 2002). The rate of maternal employment for two-parent families with school-age children is more than 75 percent. African-American women with school-age children are more likely to be employed than white or Latinas with children (Vandell & Ramanan, 1991).

Employed mothers constitute a heterogeneous group of women who vary in terms of age, relationship status (e.g., single, divorced, widowed, in lesbian relationships, and married), stage in the family life cycle (e.g., number and ages of children), and socioeconomic factors (Hill, et al., 2005; Ruhm, 2003). The reasons for women working outside the home are related primarily to financial needs and self-actualization (Sinacore-Guinn, 1998). Families must have two incomes to support them at a level previously achieved by one wage earner. Single, widowed, and divorced women with children must work to avoid poverty (Duncan & Brooks-Gunn, 2000). Thus, employment is not always a choice for women: it is a necessity. The question "should mothers of young children work?" contains an assumption that mothers do not have to work but simply want to, that they have a choice. Women have always had to work to support themselves and their families (Betz, in press; Dziech, chapter 1, this volume).

Employed women with children have also reported wanting to work for the social support, adult companionship, and social networks offered by workplaces (Hakim, 2006). Hyde, et al. (1995) described employment for mothers as a morale boost and a buffer against stress from family roles. What matters most is how satisfied mothers are with the choices they have made regarding integrating work and family (Gilbert, 1994), as well as the support they receive from mates, other family members, co-workers, and employers (Karsten, 2006).

Employed mothers report that their major sources of stress include managing the household, home cleaning, and caring for sick children (Bird, 1999; Dempsey, 1999; Karsten, 2006). Other problems include issues with time management, stress, and fatigue. The lack of time appears to be most accentuated in areas that are self-related: community activities, reading, hobbies, and physical fitness (Betz, in press). Instead of doing everything alone, women need help from other women and from men. Family chores and child-rearing responsibilities are not exclusively "women's work" (Hakim, 2006; Paludi, 2002).

The incompatibility between the workplace and family demands is exacerbated by a relative lack of provisions that would ease women's integration of these roles. Present conditions may be expected to produce greater potential stress and conflict among employed mothers, who still have the primary responsibility for child and elder care (Gottfried, et al., 2002). Traditional occupational policies reflect a separation of family from work life and a societal expectation that mothers remain at home to care for their children. There is a tendency for individuals to believe that equality translates into women being employed. However, working outside the home is not progress if women must also continue with full-time responsibility for housekeeping and motherhood, performing "double duty" or what Hochschild (1989) referred to as the "second shift." Thus, equality of the parenting and housekeeping roles has not been achieved (Gottfried, et al., 2002). Lotte Bailyn noted:

> We should challenge these assumptions. The concept of the ideal worker as someone who puts work above all else, and sacrifices other aspects of life, still guides most work practices. Maybe this made some sense for white middle-class families, when women were staying at home. But the working population has changed significantly. Most men and women no longer fit this pattern.

During the writing of this book, news reporter and anchor Elizabeth Vargas was featured on *The Oprah Winfrey Show* because she decided to step down as anchor of ABC's *World News Tonight* because of the difficulty of combining work with family. Since she gave birth to her second baby, Ms. Vargas returned to ABC news and is co-anchoring *20/20*. She told Ms. Winfrey that the nature of a weekly program rather than a nightly one is better for her and her family: "The difference in anchoring *20/20* is that I have a lot more flexibility. I can sort of call my own shots a tad more. With *World News Tonight* you're out the door at 8 A.M. and back in at 8 P.M., and that's non-negotiable....It's an intensely demanding job." *The Oprah Winfrey Show* polled approximately 15,000 women about work/life balance. When asked the question "Do you think parenthood is more or less stressful than it was when you were growing up?" 85 percent of employed women and 83 percent of stay-at-home moms said "More." When polled "Do you feel judged by family, friends or other moms?" 56 percent of stay-at-home moms and 43 percent of employed moms said "Yes." As another example, 83 percent of the employed women and 85 percent of the stay-at-home mothers stated that stay-at-home moms do not get the respect they deserve.

Similarly, Strassel, et al. (2006) summarized:

> So women sit behind more desks, drive more cranes, and build more computer chips. They do these jobs for longer hours. Yet women also continue to be the primary caregivers for their families. Working mothers are 83 percent more likely to take time off to care for a child than working fathers. And home life, with its soccer practices, doctor's visits, gymnastic lessons, and house repair and maintenance, is more hectic than at any time in the past. (p. 27)

In this book we review the issues identified by Bailyn and Strassel, et al., specifically the impact of employed mothers on children's achievement and social development, legislation to ease the integration of family and work roles (i.e., Family and Medical Leave Act), child care and elder care, and family-friendly policies to assist employees in integrating work and family roles. We also take a multicultural focus to these issues throughout the book.

Each of the contributors to this volume has taught, consulted, facilitated training programs, and conducted research in areas related to integrating work and family lives and/or has attempted to restructure their own businesses in keeping with family-friendly policies. They are psychologists, attorneys, management consultants, lobbyists, and academicians working within their own disciplines to help achieve balance in work and family lives. They acknowledge that interdisciplinary collaboration is necessary in understanding and dealing with the complex issues involved in family and work balance.

Thus, the chapters in this volume are interrelated; contributors highlighted several major themes that overlapped all topics, whether it is procedures that must be outlined for both employers and employees, a needed shift to a child-centered society, or the fact that work and homelife do not have to be oppositional. In addition, contributors reinforced the necessity to have bipartisan support at both the federal and state levels for specific family-care legislation.

United States Senate Resolution 210 has provided some support for this purpose. This resolution designates October as National Work and Family Month. According to this resolution, "Reducing the conflict between work and family life should be a national priority." It was co-sponsored by Senator Orrin Hatch (R-Utah) and Senator Edward Kennedy (D-Mass.). According to Senator Hatch,

> We all know that sick children recover more quickly when cared for by a parent, and our senior citizens are relying more and more on their working adult children to care for them when they are ill....Americans need to have the

reassurance that they can draw a healthy line, a healthy boundary, between their families and their jobs, caring for both their loved ones and their work.

Wespac Chief Executive Officer David Morgan shared this concern:

The company that helps give women control over their own lives and helps them with the things that are not working for them—by providing more flexibility, more networking opportunities, a better work environment and more challenging work—will see more women stay. It's not a compliance issue, it's not a diversity issue, and it's not a social responsibility issue. Yes, it's the right thing to do, but it's also the strategic thing to do.

We add that it is the only and necessary thing to do. The insights and recommendations offered by the contributors to this volume empowered us. We hope you also feel inspired by reading this volume to become advocates at your own workplaces on behalf of integrating work and family lives.

References

Betz, N. (in press). Career development. In F. Denmark & M. Paludi (Eds.), *Psychology of women: A handbook of issues and theories. 2ed.* Westport, CT: Praeger.

Bird, C. (1999). Gender, household labor, and psychological distress: The impact of the amount and division of housework. *Journal of Health and Social Behavior, 40,* 32–45.

Brooks-Gunn, J., Han, W., & Waldfogel, J. (2002). Maternal employment and child cognitive outcomes in the first three years of life: The NICHD study of early child care. *Child Development, 73,* 1052–1072.

Clark-Stewart, A. (1993). *Daycare.* Cambridge, MA: Harvard University Press.

Dempsey, K. (1999). Attempting to explain women's perceptions of the fairness of the division of housework. *Journal of Family Studies, 5,* 3–24.

Duncan, G., & Brooks-Gunn, J. (2000). Family, poverty, welfare reform, and child development. *Child Development, 71,* 188–196.

Gilbert, L. (1994). Current perspectives on dual-career families. *Current Directions in Psychological Science, 3,* 101–105.

Gottfried, A., Gottfried, A., & Bathurst, K. (2002). Maternal and dual-earner employment status and parenting. In M. Borstein (Ed.), *Handbook of parenting. 2ed.* Mahwah, NJ: Erlbaum.

Gurchiek, K. (2007). Give us your sick: Sick-child day care centers are designed to meet the needs of working parents and their employers. *HR Magazine, 52,* 91–93.

Hakim, C. (2006). Women, careers, and work-life preferences. *British Journal of Guidance and Counselling, 34,* 279–294.

Heymann, J. (Ed.) (2000). *The widening gap: Why American working families are in jeopardy and what can be done about it.* New York: Basic Books.

Hill, J., Waldfogel, J., Brooks-Gunn, J., & Han, E.J. (2005). Maternal employment and child development: A fresh look using newer methods. *Developmental Psychology, 41,* 833–850.

Hochschild, A. (1989). *The second shift.* New York: Viking.

Hyde, J., Klein, M., Essex, M., & Clark, R. (1995). Maternity leave and women's mental health. *Psychology of Women Quarterly, 19,* 257–285.

Kanter, R.M. (1977). *Work and family in the United States: A critical review and agenda for research and policy.* New York: Russell Sage Foundation.

Karsten, M. (2006). Managerial women, minorities, and stress: Causes and consequences. In M. Karsten (Ed.), *Gender, race and ethnicity in the workplace,* pp. 238–272. Westport, CT: Praeger.

Paludi, M. (2002). *The psychology of women. 2ed.* Upper Saddle River, NJ: Prentice Hall.

Peeters, M., Montgomery, A., Bakker, A., & Schaufeli, W. (2005). Balancing work and home: How job and home demands are related to burnout. *International Journal of Stress Management, 12,* 43–61.

Ruhm, C. (2003). Parental employment and child cognitive development. *Journal of Human Resources, 39,* 155–192.

Russo, N.F. (1979). Overview: Sex roles, fertility and the motherhood mandate. *Psychology of Women Quarterly, 4,* 7–15.

Sinacore-Guinn, A. (1998). Employed mothers: Job satisfaction and self-esteem. *Canadian Journal of Counseling, 32,* 242–258.

Strassel, K., Colgan, C., & Goodman, J. (2006). *Leaving women behind: Modern families, outdated laws.* New York: Rowman & Littlefield Publishers.

Vandell, D., & Ramanan, J. (1991). Children of the national longitudinal survey of youth: Choices in after school care and child development. *Developmental Psychology, 27,* 637–643.

CHAPTER 1

Juggling Act: Parents and Employers in the Twenty-First Century

Billie Dziech

The number of publications on integrating work and family life is vast, repetitive, and occasionally contradictory. It ranges from Internet advice to lengthy articles and books crammed with descriptions of employees' life stresses and employers' anxieties about implementing family-friendly policies. Ultimately, writers of lengthy pieces add arduously documented recommendations that resemble those of their less loquacious Internet siblings, and the reader is left wondering if development of "family-friendly" policies has been and is as simple as some theorists imply.

The answer to that question is no. There is no easy way for individuals to integrate work and family responsibilities and no company policy that can guarantee absolute success for those attempting to do so. And that reality should be the starting point for any discussion of family-friendly work environments because it provides a realistic framework within which to examine issues affecting work/life balance and to strategize about policies to provide at least some relief for those juggling work and home obligations.

Defying the Myth of the Cookie-Cutter Family Policy

It is not difficult to understand why so much of the advice being offered to employers and employees seems shallow. Picture this—you are a business or factory owner exhausted by employees complaining about conflicts between family and work responsibilities. You envy competitors who boast about spectacular procedures that have transformed their workplaces into virtual paradises. So you hire a consultant who advises you to arrange a series of brainstorming (and ultimately mind-numbing) meetings with all those who will be affected when new policies are implemented. You approach these momentous gatherings with a spring in your step and a song in your heart, believing you are finally destined to discover the magic formula that will revolutionize your workplace and make you the object of adoration by your employees.

Better still, reverse the focus and assume you are an accountant or factory worker exhausted by juggling family and job responsibilities. Your children are acting out because you miss important school events, your spouse feels neglected because you are anxious and preoccupied, and you suspect your employer is unhappy with your performance. So when the company owner or factory manager announces there will be meetings to discuss the development of family-friendly procedures, you walk with a sprightlier gait and find yourself humming at the water cooler, convinced that miracles do happen and that you are about to be rescued from the depths of family/work conflict.

Whichever scenario is applicable, you might as well forget it. Miracles happen but seldom as a result of even the most well-intentioned policies. To fill space in their articles, gushy freelance writers might hyperbolize about the wonders of a particular set of procedures, but neither employers nor employees will ever be completely satisfied with any policy, regardless of the effort expended in developing it. There are perfectly rational explanations for this, even though academics and consultants who have the good fortune of dwelling in the Land of Theory seldom acknowledge the limitations of the procedures they promote. The first reason that work/family policies are never as friendly as some perceive them to be is that people are extraordinarily unique (hardly a surprise). Even basic reasons for working vary. For purposes of simplification, we might say that some work primarily out of choice, while others are employed because they must be if they wish to survive.

"Choice" can have a number of implications. Some people work because they like being occupied and/or are stimulated by the tasks they perform. Contrary to the common assumption that people prefer to remain at home, some researchers have contended that women who work are less likely to be depressed, have higher self-esteem, and feel greater control and satisfaction in their lives (Baruch, Biener, & Barnett, 1987). In a study of AMERCO's family-friendly reforms, Hochschild concluded that she discovered a "new model of family and work life" in which "a tired parent flees a world of unresolved quarrels and unwashed laundry for the reliable orderliness, harmony, and managed cheer of work. The emotional magnets beneath home and workplace are in the process of being reversed" (Hochschild, 1987).

Since research has reached so many different conclusions about attitudes toward employment, it is obvious that no single outlook exists. But the implications with regard to workplace policies are nevertheless clear. If, like Charles Baudelaire, you believe work "strengthens us" (www. quotationspage.com), most accommodations for family life will sound beneficial and will probably meet with your approval—until a family crisis arises and your company's policy is not generous enough. But if you have adopted Oscar Wilde's point of view and consider work "the refuge of people who have nothing else to do"(www.quotationspage.com), any policy will seem less than friendly—even without a family crisis. And if you must oversee individuals with these diametrically opposed attitudes, you yourself will undoubtedly find the workplace inhospitable at times.

But do not be discouraged. At least not yet. Beyond differing assumptions about work, there are additional complications or myths about designing perfect procedures. One of the most common is the assumption that every "family" is identical. The absurdity of that notion is apparent if one considers simply a few characteristics of two-parent families with children. Three-fifths of all traditional families in 2000 had two wage earners (Jacobs & Gerson, 2004c), but few were identical. For instance, families with one child obviously have fewer supervisory responsibilities than those with two or more children. U.S. Census data support this observation. In 2000, couples with one child younger than 18 jointly averaged eighty-one hours of work a week, while those with three or more children worked an average of seventy-eight hours per week (Jacobs & Gerson, 2004c). Parents with several children have been known to remark that the potential for stress and conflict increases in geometric proportion as more members are added to the family.

Children in some traditional families are engaged in several school and extracurricular activities that require parents to function as chauffeurs and spectators, while sedentary youth in other two-parent families prefer to spend spare time with their computers or television sets. Some traditional parents live near family and/or friends who are willing to provide daily support or aid in crises. Others are far from family and have no help with routine obligations, illnesses, and emergencies. Some spouses are responsible for aging or ill relatives or friends, in contrast to those who have only immediate family duties. Lengthy commutes to and from work reduce some parents' time with families, while others are employed in close proximity to work, homes, and schools. Some employers require no travel, and other families are forced to make accommodations for parents whose careers demand frequent time away from home.

These limited examples should sufficiently illustrate a crucial point, which is that the workers in an organization can be characterized by seemingly inexhaustible variables. But this is only the beginning of the complexity in defining family. The term applies to single-parent as well as two-parent households. In 2000, one-fifth of all families were headed by women. This is twice the 1970 percentage (Jacobs & Gerson, 2004c). Although there are far fewer single-parent fathers, they too face unique and daunting challenges at home and in the workplace. Then there are divorced parents with shared custody, a relatively new familial arrangement with substantial challenges of its own. Clearly then, this complicated mix proves there can never be a "one-size-fits-all" approach to addressing the needs and desires of every worker in an organization.

A similar observation can be made about employers. Cookie-cutter procedures are often as infeasible for them as for their employees. For example, companies that operate on erratic as opposed to consistent schedules or have production constraints will not be able to meet deadlines if family policies are too restrictive. The same is true of businesses that engage in competition; their profits will suffer if no provisions exist for workplace, as well as employee, emergencies. Then too policies must take into account fluctuations in the labor market. This is an especially important concern for the very near future when the replacements for retiring Baby Boomers will come from Generation X, a much smaller generation.

There are institutions and corporations that employ hundreds and even thousands of individuals with vastly different credentials and duties, and they too are limited in the types of procedures they can offer. Colleges and universities provide one of the clearest illustrations of the dissatisfaction that exists below the surface and occasionally in the open when individuals with divergent functions and professional life-styles work in close contact. "Nine-to-five" employees seldom understand or accept the seemingly privileged comings and goings of professors any more than faculty members approve of what they perceive to be the "globe-trotting" life-styles of college administrators. Each group performs totally different services on vastly different time lines, so there is no way to establish a one-size-fits-all policy for such divergent groups.

Discussions of family policies tend to focus on workers' interests, but it is crucial to recognize that because an employer's needs and priorities often run counter to those of employees, procedures must be formulated with give and take from both sides. One of writer André Gide's characters in *The Counterfeiters* identifies the mutual understanding that is needed when he observes, "I said to myself that nothing is good for everyone, but only relatively to some people; that nothing is true for everyone, but only to the person who believes it is; that there is no method and no theory which can be applied indifferently to all alike" (1927). This being the case, the challenge is to accept that family-friendly policies cannot be written in stone. Instead they should always be "in process" and open to reconsideration and change as circumstances, needs, and priorities alter over time.

History and Gender Politics in the Workplace

But infinite workforce diversity is not the only problem confronting those who wish to create more hospitable environments for employees. Since family concerns are integrally related to gender issues, another challenge is recognizing the gender prejudices and confusion that once characterized work environments and may still influence responses to organizational decision making. Workplace culture evolved, at least in part, from the influence of individuals like the nineteenth century philosopher Arthur Schopenhauer whose assessment of women was less than complimentary: "You need only to look at the way in which she is formed to see that woman is not meant to undergo great labor, whether of the mind or of the body....Women are directly fitted for acting as the nurses and teachers of our early childhood by the fact that they are themselves childish, frivolous, and shortsighted; in a word, they are big children all their life long" (1928).

His observations of the opposite sex led him to conclude, "[Women] are dependent, not upon strength, but upon craft; and hence their instinctive capacity for cunning, and their ineradicable tendency to say what is not true. ...Now when the laws gave women equal rights with man, they ought also to have endowed her with a masculine intellect....The people who make money are men, not women; and it follows from this that women are neither justified in having unconditional possession of it, not fit persons to be entrusted with its administration....That woman is by nature meant to obey man may be seen in the fact that every woman who is placed in the unnatural position of complete independence immediately attaches herself to some man, by whom she allows herself to be guided and ruled. It is because she needs a lord and master" (Schopenhauer, 1928).

Seldom one to mince words himself, Sigmund Freud did little to help the female image when he proclaimed, "The great question that has never been answered, and which I have not yet been able to answer, despite my thirty years of research into the feminine soul, is 'What does a woman want?'" (www.quotationspage.com). So much for philosophers and psychoanalysts.... Given such influences, it should come as no surprise that even now employers continue to express uncertainty about how to deal with these "big children" who are transforming the workplace at the same time they are caring for children and homes and fulfilling what Schopenhauer described as their additional duty—being "patient and cheering companions" (1928) to spouses.

Some forget or are unaware that matriarchal societies once existed and that women, in the aggregate, have always worked and contributed to their families' survival. In the earliest preindustrial societies, females gathered food, maintained living quarters, and cared for others while males hunted. This division of labor was a practical one, influenced by the necessity for women to reproduce in small societies where survival was always in question. The physical demands and dangers of hunting meant that it was more practical for those who were pregnant, nursing, or capable of reproducing to remain in safer, more stable environments. So important were the contributions of females in these hunter-gatherer societies that subsequent generations of researchers have contended they experienced greater equality with males than at any other period in history (Yorburg, 1987).

Gradual technological advances brought changes in the lives of both sexes. As inventions like the plow led to crop surpluses that could be traded or purchased, men began to engage in increasingly specialized work outside the home, while women's tasks included a complex set of activities such as providing food, clothing, child care, cleaning, medical aid, education, religious instruction, and support in maintaining crops and property (Yorburg, 1987).

With the advent of industrialization, needy women from minorities and the lower classes demonstrated females' abilities to work in even the most undesirable factory environments where they were poorly paid and given none of the opportunities available to men. Immigrants and others from the working class were often employed as servants in the homes of the wealthy. Although they were at first regarded with hesitation, eligible white women were permitted to assume additional roles as teachers, nurses, and secretaries. Many or most of these working women had domestic and child-care responsibilities as well. Those who were lucky enough not to suffer economic disadvantage were nevertheless responsible for oversight of homes and care for children and others in need (Matthaei, 1982).

But it was World War II that forever disproved the notion of females as big children unfit for physical or mental exertion. Women in the 1940s knew exactly what they wanted and needed to do when American males marched off to war and severe labor shortages threatened. Thousands took over crucial jobs in factories where they succeeded in performing as well as men (Kemp, 1994), and still others traveled across the ocean to serve in the armed services.

When the war ended and men resumed their previous positions, women were displaced—but not for long. They began to enter the workplace in larger and larger numbers so that by 1950, they constituted 29.6 percent of the labor force as opposed to 18.3 percent in 1900 and 24.3 percent in 1940 (Kemp, 1994). The percentages continued to rise, and by 1970, women's share of the labor force was 38.1 percent (Kemp, 1994). By 2000, that number would rise to 46.5 percent of the workforce; and in 2003, the latest year for which information is available, women's participation was still increasing, in this case to 46.6 percent (Kemp, 1994). The reasons for their increased participation were numerous. Rising divorce rates forced mothers to contribute to support of their children; some sought employment because they recognized the risks of becoming financially dependent on males (Matthaei, 1982); and growing similarities in the genders' educational achievements meant more attractive employment opportunities for women. Then too females were the primary beneficiaries of federal legislation.

Although the Fair Labor Standards Act was not passed until 1938, years of abysmal conditions in factories and sweatshops led to the law that protected workers' health and improved their working conditions and pay (Sterling, 1996). When it was finally enacted, it applied to both sexes and established a minimum wage and a forty-four-hour maximum workweek (Sterling, 1996). The next major legislation, the Equal Pay Act, was passed in 1963 and prohibited employers from paying women less than men for the same job. A year later, Title VII of the Civil Rights Act barred discrimination in employment on the basis of sex and race, and the Equal Employment Opportunity Commission (EEOC) was created to enforce Title VII and to monitor workplace practices and help prevent discrimination.

But the most revolutionary—and controversial—legislation was that pertaining to sexual harassment. Although the term itself was not invented until the 1970s, women were especially familiar with and subjected to the behavior from the time the first female entered a work environment. When legislation to improve work environments was implemented, most people could understand why decent working conditions were necessary; and eventually even the concept of equal pay for equal work became acceptable, particularly in the cases of women who were providing support for families. But it was much more difficult to convince society that sexual harassment was a valid problem.

Nevertheless, the Supreme Court legitimized the issue in the 1976 case of *Williams v. Saxbe*. It established the foundation for "quid pro quo" sexual harassment by finding that individuals deserved remedy under the law for submitting to employers' sexual demands when a particular "pattern of conduct" results in an "artificial barrier to employment." Convincing some of the validity of the legislation was not easy. "She asked for it" and "she should have known better" were familiar refrains in cultures that assumed "boys would be boys," and females with families probably suffered most in bringing claims because these prejudices encouraged others to view victims' husbands and children as the real casualties of sex in the workplace.

The concept of "hostile environment" harassment was an even harder "sell" four years later when the EEOC followed developing court trends by including in its 1980 Guidelines on Discrimination because of Sex "conduct [that] has the purpose or effect of substantially interfering with an individual's work performance or creating an intimidating, hostile, or offensive work environment" (Equal Employment Opportunity Commission, 1990). Additional guidelines that followed placed greater and greater responsibility on employers at the same time the Court did not clarify employers' and lower courts' uncertainties about the issue.

The links between the harassment issue and concerns about accommodations for workers with families were—and are—strong. Many of those who never accepted sexual harassment as a valid problem also regarded the family issue as "bogus," and no amount of persuasion could convince them that women faced special challenges in attempting to juggle work and family obligations. This was true in spite of research conducted by people like Hochschild, who studied discrepancies between the lives of married parents who worked during the 1960s and 1970s. She subsequently coined the term "second shift" to describe women's lives during those years.

> Adding together the time it takes to do a paid job and to do housework and childcare, I averaged estimates from the major studies on time use done in the 1960s and 1970s and discovered that women worked roughly fifteen hours longer each week than men. Over a year, they worked an extra month of twenty-four hour days a year. Over a dozen years, it was an extra year of twenty-four hour days. Most women without children spend much more time on housework; with children, they devote more time to both housework and childcare. Just as there is a wage gap between men and women in the workplace, there is a "leisure gap" between them at home. Most women work one shift at the office or factory and a "second shift" at home. (Hochschild, 1987)

If it were possible to design family policies to meet only women's experiences and perceptions, the task would be much easier. But over time it has
become apparent that men also bring personal and historical memories to
the workplace and that these too are relevant to discussions of family policies.
The "second wave" of the Women's Movement, which began in the 1960s
and 1970s, provides one illustration of the impact that words can have on
relations between the sexes. It was often characterized by rhetoric from feminists that were as hostile to males as Schopenhauer was to females.

Ms. Magazine editor Robin Morgan declared, "I feel that 'man-hating' is an
honorable and viable political act, that the oppressed have a right to class-
hatred against the class that is oppressing them" (http://wiki:
mensactivism.org). Radical feminist writer Andrea Dworkin was even
more direct: "I want to see a man beaten to a bloody pulp with a high-heel
shoved in his mouth, like an apple in the mouth of a pig" (http://wiki:
mensactivism.org). Author Marilyn French concluded, "My feelings about
men are the result of my experience. I have little sympathy for them. Like a
Jew just released from Dachau, I watch the handsome young Nazi soldier fall
writhing to the ground with a bullet in his stomach, and I look briefly and
walk on. I don't even need to shrug. I simply don't care" (http://wiki:
mensactivism.org). Congresswoman Barbara Jordan's denigration of males
bore similarities to that of Schopenhauer's disparagement of females: "I
believe that women have a capacity for understanding and compassion which
man structurally does not have, does not have because he cannot have it. He's
just incapable of it" (http://wiki:mensactivism.org). Author and college professor Mary Daly was even more derogatory: "If life is to survive on this
planet, there must be a decontamination of the Earth. I think this will be
accompanied by an evolutionary process that will result in a drastic reduction
of the population of males" (http://wiki:mensactivism.org).

To say that all women agree with these views would be as irresponsible as
maintaining that all men considered women inferior. The Women's Movement was "on a roll," however, and the media spotlighted its more extreme
representatives so that many males became convinced that they were being
punished or made to "pay for history" (Dziech, 1995). Frequently they
reacted with defensiveness and animosity. If Affirmative Action initiatives
meant for women a long-awaited chance to "level the playing field," males
often saw them as threats to their careers and attempts to diminish them
and their values. If women were the more likely victims of sexual harassment
in the workplace, they reasoned, men more frequently died from work-
related mishaps. If women had to work "second shifts" and suffered because
of "deadbeat dads," fathers were equally pained by having no say in decisions
about whether their children should be aborted or in custody cases where
gender stereotyping usually favored mothers.

Such debates were bitter and agonizing for the segment of the male population that felt the future held more peril than promise. Forced to consider
"what women might want" in life, others began to question society's expec-

tations for them as well as women and to reflect on their own priorities and life-styles. They reasoned that if women could redefine themselves, their values, and their places in the world, then perhaps male roles also demanded reassessment. Given the two extremes, predictions about family/workplace policies would have been at best speculative.

Changing Times

Nevertheless, just beneath the surface lay a new force that eventually altered the office and factory landscape and drew working men and women closer than might have been predicted after the heightened rhetoric of the 1960s and 1970s. The Food and Drug Administration approved the birth control pill in 1960; and as the Women's Movement gathered momentum, birthrates began to decline. The drop had already begun in 1958; and by 1968, the United States experienced its longest "baby bust" in history. Rising abortion rates in the 1970s clearly indicated that babies and children had ceased to be focal points for Americans, as the proportionally smallest generation in history was born between 1965 and the early to mid-1980s. Ultimately labeled "Generation X" or the "Latch-key Generation," this group was the product of parents who subscribed to the advice that "quality" mattered more than "quantity" time in rearing children. Popular culture reflected little interest in the very young as subjects for film, television, music, and literature; and the market demonstrated only average interest in children and teens.

Identifying the exact point at which change emerged is as difficult as explaining why it occurred at all, and an explanation is probably not relevant to this discussion. What can be unequivocally stated, however, is that between the early and mid-1980s, Americans suddenly began to alter course and concentrate on children. Tots through teens could boast not only their own designer fashion lines but also clothing, toy, and entertainment stores devoted exclusively to them. Babies and toddlers, "kids" and teens were suddenly everywhere—on the covers of magazines and on television and movie screens. As time passed, producers discovered the monetary magic of not only films marketed to adolescent audiences but also of "family" movies like *Three Men and a Baby* and *Sleepless in Seattle*. Studios like Walt Disney revived what had seemed to be a moribund animation market with soon-to-be classics like *The Lion King* and *The Little Mermaid*, and a television industry for toddlers gradually emerged.

Over time politicians "got the message." Conservatives campaigned for "family values" and liberals for "villages" in which to rear children, but the underlying message was really the same—kids were "in" again; and that meant a change in both adult life-styles and finances. The recipients of all this attention were a totally unique group of Americans. Born between the 1980s and the end of the twentieth century, Millennials (also labeled Generation Y or Gen Y), would eventually become the largest and wealthiest generation in United States history (Howe & Strauss, 2000).

By 2003, a Harris Interactive YouthPulse study revealed that there were 57 million 8- to 21-year-olds and that they spent approximately $172 billion a year. A stroll through any upscale mall or a Wal-Mart confirms the affluence of American youth, who have extraordinary amounts to spend on clothing, entertainment, gadgets, hobbies, and expensive electronic equipment, so much so that they have become one of the driving forces in the nation's economy. One Harris researcher noted, "Generation Y's needs and opinions drive many adult purchase decisions, and they, literally, represent the future market for most consumer brands" (Harris Interactive YouthPulse, 2003).

But the emergence of a child-centered culture meant also creation of an exceptionally expensive "child improvement industry" that costs average parents as much or more than their investments in "things" for their off-spring. Every year Baby Boomers and Gen Xers old enough to have Millennial children spend greater and greater sums to ensure their children excel socially, physically, and academically. Sports equipment and camps; dancing, cheerleading, and gymnastics lessons; SAT preparation classes; orthodontia; dermatology—many are no longer luxuries of the wealthy but have become necessities that even less affluent parents seek and, through additional work, acquire for their children.

So how does this emphasis on the young affect the workplace? In more ways than the average person knows. The shift to a child-centered society requires enormous investments of time and energy, as well as money; and even the most idealistic working mothers eventually began to question the validity of the superwoman image with which they were once infected. Work became increasingly less optional for women as parents spent more and more to ensure their children were successful and happy. In 1970, 50 percent of all two-parent households were supported only by males. By 2000, only 25 percent belonged in that category (Jacobs & Gerson, 2004c). At the same time families felt compelled to earn more, they were also faced with greater demands on their time and energy. Distressed by the poor academic performance of many Gen Xers, educators adopted zero-tolerance policies for underachievers. This meant more homework and increased pressure on adults to oversee and assist children. Along with astronomical tuition increases came fierce competition for admissions to even some community colleges, and already stressed parents felt obliged to intensify the oversight and assistance process with teenagers, many of whom were enrolled in high school classes beyond the educational levels of their parents.

Baby Boomers and older generations can usually cite long weekend and summer days when they had nothing to do but dream or create their own recreation. Not any more. Baseball in the latter years of the last century, as now, was followed by soccer and/or football, succeeded by basketball and/or volleyball. Then the process begins again. Many of these kinds of activities begin at younger and younger ages and take more and more time. Someone has to provide transportation to and from games and practices. Generally that someone is assumed to be a parent, who is expected to supply refreshments at a designated time, cheer the children, and man the carpool when his or her turn comes. That is, if the parent is not working; and if he or she is doing so, you can be sure that feelings of guilt lurk in every corner of the workplace.

But transportation woes were and are the tip of the iceberg for parents. The massacre at Columbine High School became for Millennials a watershed event, one of the incidents they themselves invariably cite as most vivid in their memories. Baby Boomer parents and teachers probably remember it with even more apprehension. Since then other highly publicized school shootings have left parents extraordinarily anxious about their children's safety, and seemingly unending accounts of child molestations have exacerbated public perception of the dangers young people confront in the world. The result, fortunately, has been parental awareness of the importance of protecting the young. But someone has to provide the protection. After school programs and daycare cost money that many working families struggle to afford, so parents are forced to juggle work and childcare obligations.

If a sizable number of males were oblivious to the complexities of child care and household maintenance prior to the arrival of the Millennials, there appeared to be greater awareness as economic and time pressures increased. In 1965, the ratio of women's to men's involvement in housework was six to one, but by the mid-1990s, it had declined to a ratio of almost two to one (Bianchi, Milkie, Sayer, & Robinson, 2000). Nevertheless, women remained primarily responsible for house maintenance. One study estimated that while males in working families spent an average of 10.4 hours a week on household tasks, women contributed 19.4 hours (Kunz Center, 1998).

One Step Forward: The Family and Medical Leave Act

In any case, as both working men and working women reported increasing stress, politicians were forced to respond. Many corporations had, by the 1990s, already incorporated family-friendly policies. Then in 1993, the Family and Medical Leave Act (FMLA) was signed into law after almost a decade of debate and negotiation. The major federal initiative to respond to the caregiving needs of working families, the FMLA applies to "public agencies, including state, local and federal employers, local education agencies (schools), and private-sector employers who employed fifty or more employees in twenty or more workweeks in the current or preceding calendar year and who are engaged in commerce or in any industry or activity affecting commerce—including joint employers and successors of covered employers."

The legislation guarantees that workers employed for more than twelve months or 1,250 hours within seventy-five miles of the workplace can take up to twelve weeks of unpaid leave per year without losing their jobs to care for newborn and newly adopted infants and seriously ill children, spouses, or parents. In 1997, the federal government extended coverage to include time off to participate in children's school activities related to educational achievements and to accompany elderly relatives to professional appointments.

In addition to allowing employees time to care for others, the legislation also provides leave for workers to recover from their own serious health conditions. "Serious health condition" is defined in lengthy terminology that essentially pertains to those requiring treatment of at least one night in a "hospital, hospice, or residential medical-care facility and any period of incapacity or subsequent treatment in connection with such inpatient care" and to those requiring "continuing treatment by a health care provider which includes any period of incapacity" due to one of several causes, including pregnancy.

In addition to enacting the FMLA in 1993, Congress also established the Commission on Leave, which was assigned the task of evaluating issues surrounding the legislation and its impact. In 1995 and again in 2000, the University of Michigan conducted surveys of employees, while Westat surveyed employers. The 2000 results are summarized by Waldfogel (1997). This report includes "tips" that should help both employers and their employees assess their work environments.

> 83.7% of establishments covered by FMLA provided all benefits it mandates, whereas only 33.5% of establishments not covered offered all five. But the gap is narrowing, and establishments not covered by law are far more likely to provide benefits in 2000 than they were five years earlier. Although approximately two-thirds of employers find the FMLA easy to administer, more reported difficulties in 2000 than in 1995. A sizable minority of both covered and uncovered establishments is offering leave beyond that mandated by the FMLA. The median length of leave in 2000 was ten days; about 90% were for 12 or fewer weeks. About 97% of employers cover the work of leave takers by assigning it temporarily to other employees, and the majority of businesses covered by the FMLA reported that it had no noticeable effects on productivity, profitability, and growth.
>
> Only about 16.5% of employees used the FMLA in the year and a half prior to the survey. Employees were most likely to take leaves for their own health needs (47.2%). Provision of care for newborns, newly adopted or newly placed foster children was the second most cited reason (17.9%); 34.1% of men and 35.8% of women with young children took leaves for these reasons. In the eighteen months prior to the survey 75.8% of women and 45.1% of men with young children took some form of leave.
>
> Employees indicated significant satisfaction with family and medical leave. Reasons offered were that it had positive effects on their abilities to care for family members (78.7%) and/or their own or family members' emotional (70.1%) or physical (63.0%) health. A large majority (93.5%) responded that leave helped them to comply with doctors' instructions and that it led to quicker recovery (83.7%).

Most (72.6%) reported satisfaction with the amount of leave time available, although the percentage of "very satisfied" respondents dropped to 42.2% in 2000 from 48.2% in 1995.

The most serious concern of leave takers (53.8%) was financial; 58.2% who did not receive full or any pay during leave found it somewhat or very difficult to meet financial obligations, and 50.9% said they would have taken longer leaves if money had not been an issue.

The two most pressing problem areas are making provision for some sort of paid leaves and providing leaves to those not currently covered or eligible.

Critics of the FMLA have expressed concerns about specific constituencies. Elison (1997), for example, argued that the law "is targeted to cover those within the primary sector of the labor market who are more likely to have access to financial and familial resources." Cockerham (1995) maintained that African-Americans were disadvantaged because they have higher rates of morbidity and health problems and because they define family in wider terms than the legislation. Others noted that since 79 percent of single mothers are employed (Bureau of Labor Statistics, 2005), they suffer additional economic burdens that discourage leave taking. Still others observed that individuals in managerial and professional roles are less likely to take advantage of the FMLA because their employers have made higher investments in hiring, training, and promoting them so they work longer hours, are more responsive to workplace cultures that demand continuous availability, and feel greater organizational commitment (Jacobs & Gerson, 2004a).

Some suggest that family-friendly leaves may not, in actuality, be all that "friendly." A considerable body of research contends that employees tend to refuse leave opportunities because they fear negative impact on salaries and/or job mobility (Fried, 1998; Golden, 2001; Hochschild, 1997). While some research confirms that leaves have positive effects on women's employment (e.g., reduced turnover, improved morale, and greater loyalty) (Glass and Riley, 1998; Waldfogel, 1997), other reports express concern that males who take leaves are likely to be viewed negatively in the workplace (Wayne & Cordeiro, 2003). Still other research maintains that performance ratings, promotions, salary increases, and merit pay often suffer in the short term (Judiesch & Lyness, 1999).

Perhaps the most reliable concern expressed about the legislation is that while it mandates certain procedures, it can demand only that an employer and employees abide by the law. It cannot ensure that legal procedures or company policies will change organizational culture. All in all, research findings on the FMLA are so varied that in some cases it is difficult to draw sound conclusions because almost everyone who has a stake in the concept of leave taking or a personal or political affinity with some group of stakeholders desires additions or changes in the legislation. At the same time the legislation was an important step forward, it was also one more reminder that "one-size" approaches can never "fit all."

The Workplace of the Twenty-First Century

Nowhere is this reality more obvious than in comparing previous generations of working men and women with those of Gen X. When the American Business Collaboration (ABC) commissioned the Families and Work Institute to prepare a report in 2002 on "a new generation at work," the findings were clear: there are considerable differences in the values of Generation X when compared to those of Baby Boomers. (In this chapter the report's statistics on Generation Y and the generation preceding the Baby Boomers are not included because Boomers and Gen X comprise the largest working populations at present.) The report found that 22 percent of Boomers are "work centric," a term that means they place a higher priority on work demands than on those of family. Only 12 percent of Generation X workers, on the other hand, fit this description, and 52 percent of them can be described as "family centric" instead. In contrast, 41 percent of Baby Boomers place a higher priority on family.

In some respects, the most interesting changes appear to have occurred in males. The survey found that Gen X mothers are spending approximately the same amount of time per workday as they did in the 1970s, a fact that led the researchers to conclude that children today are receiving more attention than their counterparts in 1977 because fathers spend an average of one hour more each workday with their children, even though they work more paid and unpaid hours a week (45.6 average) than employees of similar ages in 1977 (42.9 average). The study concluded that "work-family issues are clearly family issues, not just women's issues" (Families and Work Institute, 2002).

Especially important for employers to consider is that the desire to assume more responsibility and advance in jobs has declined dramatically among all age groups in the period from 1992 to 2002. In 1992, 80 percent of all workers under 23 expressed a desire to have positions with more responsibility; ten years later that statistic had dropped to 60 percent. For workers between the ages of 23 and 37, the decline was 15 points. In 1992, 69 percent wanted "to get ahead," while only 54 percent expressed a desire for more responsibility in 2002.

The decline was especially dramatic among college-educated men and women. During this decade there was a decline of 16 percentage points among males who want to move into higher positions (68 percent in 1992 to 52 percent in 2002). College-educated women evidenced an even sharper contrast; in 1992, 57 percent wanted to advance to more responsible positions. In 2002, that number declined by 21 percentage points to 36 percent. The researchers view this downward trend in ambition as "the real revolution" in which hardworking men and women are no longer willing to make the trade-offs necessary for advancement.

So how does one explain this phenomenon? The report theorizes that the younger generation is not less willing to work hard, but that the problems arise when work hours "consistently exceed personally acceptable levels"

(Families and Work Institute, 2002). The researchers conclude that members of this group "have seen their parents or other adults put everything into work only to lose their jobs as wave after wave of downsizing hit the economy during their growing-up years. . . . They have seen the notion of a job-for-life replaced by the notion of 'employment at will,' where employers are less loyal to employees whom they see as 'free agents' responsible for their own 'employability.' Furthermore, today's younger employees have seen work become more and more demanding as the 24/7 global economy has taken hold. Finally, they have been shaped by September 11, 2001, which caused many people to step back and ask themselves what is truly important in their lives" (Families and Work Institute, 2002).

Additional research suggests that the situation appears unlikely to change among Millennials as they assume control of the workforce. The latest survey published by the Higher Education Research Institute (HERI) at the University of California/Los Angeles (2006) demonstrates that the objective the matriculating class of 2005 considers second most crucial in life is "being well off financially" (74.5 percent). Males placed only a slightly higher priority on this goal (75.9 percent to females' 73.4 percent). The group also responded that its second and third most important reasons for going to college were "to be able to get a better job" (72.2 percent) and "to be able to make more money" (71.0 percent). But having a good job, making money, and being well off financially can all be linked to the goal the students identified as more "essential or very important" than any other; 75.9 percent said it was "raising families" (males, 75.2 percent; females, 76.4 percent).

There are two other measures that suggest students are not particularly driven by the need for work-centric lives. Only 47.3 percent of males and 39.7 percent of females said they felt strongly about "becoming successful in businesses of their own"; and even smaller percentages, 42.6 percent of men and 38.6 percent of women, considered "having administrative responsibility for the work of others" essential or very important. Interestingly, both genders retain confidence in the American work ethic; males "agreed strongly or somewhat" that "through hard work, everybody can succeed in American society." Females expressed an almost identical opinion (78.4 percent).

The optimal workplace is one where employees are "dual centric" and capable of understanding and respecting differences between generations and their abilities and attitudes toward work and family. In such cases, the generations can benefit from sharing knowledge, skills, and experience in the work environment. Younger employees, for instance, are generally more knowledgeable about technology, whereas older workers bring a wealth of information about the values and politics of organizations.

One final but essential point that those concerned about tomorrow's workplace must bear in mind is the emerging gender gap. It has the potential to revolutionize the American family and workforce in ways we may not currently be able to predict. For decades females have been increasing their numbers in higher education. Today and in projections for the foreseeable future, their enrollment and graduation rates exceed those of males in surprising proportions. In 1995, for example, there were 7,919,200 women enrolled in higher education institutions as opposed to 6,342,500 males. By 2004, females outnumbered males by even greater amount—9,884,800 to 7,387,300; and the Department of Education projects that by 2014, those figures will increase to 11,386,000 women students to 8,084 men.

Current and future female students will receive significantly more associate, bachelor's, and master's degrees than males. In 2006, men are projected to earn 25,100 doctorates as opposed to women's 23,300; but by 2014, females will be ahead 27,600 to 27,300. Possibly more significant is that women already obtain more first-professional degrees; in 2006, they are predicted to earn 44,900 such degrees to men's 42,700. Projections are that by 2014, that number will rise to 53,700 compared to males' 47,300.

As theoretical as many of these numbers may sound, they possess clear and urgent messages for all types of employers; not only must they discover ways to compete and/or provide services in a complex, often international economy without disadvantaging either themselves or their employees, they must also adjust to a radically altered workforce and an inevitably changing workplace culture.

Working women, for example, will increase in number; and better education and sheer numbers will give them louder voices and greater negotiating power. They will be supported by husbands and co-workers as never before. (According to the ABC report, in 1997, only 34 percent of Baby Boomers disagreed that women should stay at home and care for the children while men earned the income; in 2002, 58 percent of the same group disagreed. Percentages of disagreement by Generations X and Y are even higher.) Clearly males have grown less threatened by female competition and more desirous of greater family/work balance.

Bond, Galinsky, Kim, and Brownfield (2005) describe their 2005 *National Study of Employers* (NSE) as the "most comprehensive and far-reaching study of the practices, policies, programs, and benefits provided by U.S. employers to address the changing needs of today's workforce and workplace." Funded by the Alfred P. Sloan Foundation, NSE found that despite fluctuations in the economy, work/family policies continue to be maintained and even increased as the workforce grows and becomes more diverse. Employees paid a greater proportion of health benefits in 2005 than in 1998, and employers were somewhat less likely to contribute to retirement plans and offer full pay leaves for new mothers, but the report indicated that cutbacks were the result of direct cost problems for employers.

The NSE survey confirmed other studies that found leaves of absence, programs for parents of young children and teenagers, elder care assistance, flexibility, and, most crucial, health care assistance to both employers and employees to be common. It reported that policies regarding leaves of absence have remained the same since 1998, with the exception of fathers being allowed longer leaves after the addition of children to their families. The FMLA has, of course, accounted for this change. The single most important worker benefit, health insurance coverage by employers of 100 or more, has not declined: 98 percent offer full-time employees coverage; 94 percent, family benefits; and 38 percent full or prorated benefits for part-time employees. With respect to other work/family initiatives, the greatest changes have been in employers being more responsible about notifying workers of resources.

According to the NSE, the one exception has been that many organizations still do not do all they can to support workplace flexibility. Two no- or low-cost initiatives that employers can adopt would be to improve efforts to inform employees about assistance for managing work and family obligations and to measure workers' performance by their achievements rather than the number of hours they spend in the workplace. Flexibility or flextime can include at least seven options: allowing workers periodical changes in starting and quitting times, allowing such changes daily, permitting employees to remain in the same position while moving between part- and full-time work, permitting job sharing, allowing compressed workweeks, permitting employees to work at home or off-site on a regular basis, and allowing workers to return gradually after childbirth. Researchers found that between 1998 and 2005, there were no significant decreases in flexibility offerings in the companies they studied and that there were increases in daily flextime and in compressed workweeks.

One interesting finding of the report is that smaller employers, those with 50–99 employees nationwide, are far more likely to provide flexibility to all or most employees than larger organizations. In no cases are they less likely to do so. Almost all studies have found that despite their limitations and inability to comply completely with individual demands, flexible scheduling, family leave, and other family-friendly initiatives do improve morale, encourage employee loyalty, and reduce turnover (Glass & Riley, 1998; Waldfogel, 1997). In the long run, they are worth the time, the energy, and the short-term economic costs that employers expend.

On the brink of the twenty-first century, American employers and employees face transitions that few could have predicted even a quarter century ago. Both will confront significant challenges. They will be called upon to adjust to even greater change, to remain productive in an increasingly competitive society, and to value and protect family life as never before. There will be no easy or ultimate solutions to the difficulties and demands that lie ahead. But impressive progress has already occurred. It reminds us that men and women, employers and employees, work and home are not oppositional forces and that together we are capable of discovering balance and fulfillment in our lives.

Selected Bibliography

Allen, T.D., & Russell, J.E. (1999). Parental leave of absence: Some not so family-friendly implications. *Journal of Applied Social Psychology, 2,* 166–191.

Anderson, K. (1988). A history of women's work in the U.S. In A. Stromberg & S. Harkness (Eds.), *Women working,* 2nd Edition. Mountain View, CA: Mayfield Publishing.

Baruch, G., Biener, L., & Barnett, R.C. (1987). Women and gender in research on work and family stress. *American Psychologist, 4,* 130–136.

Bianchi, S.M., Milkie, M.A., Sayer, L.C., & Robinson, J.P. (2000). Is anyone doing the housework? Trends in the division of household labor. *Social Forces, 7,* 191–228.

Bond, J.T., Galinsky, E., Kim, S.S., & Brownfield, E. (2005). *National study of employers: Highlights and findings.* New York: Families and Work Institute.

Bureau of Labor Statistics (2005). *Women in the labor force: A databook.* Washington, DC: www.bls.gov/cps/wlf-databook2005.htm.

CIRP Freshman Survey (2006). In *The American freshman: National norms for 2005.* Los Angeles, CA: Los Angeles-Cooperative Institutional Research Program of the Higher Education Research Institute of the University of California.

Cockerham, W. (1995). *Medical sociology.* Englewood Cliffs, NJ: Prentice Hall.

Cooperative Institutional Research Program of the Higher Education Research Institute of the University of California, Los Angeles (2006). *The American freshman: National norms for Fall 2005.*

Dziech, B.W. (1995). Coping with the alienation of white male students. *The Chronicle of Higher Education, 41,* B1–B2.

Dziech, B., & Hawkins, M. (1998). *Sexual harassment in higher education.* New York: Garland Press.

Elison, S.K. (1997). The Family and Medical Leave Act of 1993. *Journal of Family Issues, 18,* 30–54.

Equal Employment Opportunity Commission (1990). *Policy guidance on sexual harassment.*

Estes, S.B., & Glass, J. (1996). Job changes following childbirth. *Work and Occupations, 23,* 405–436.

Family and Medical Leave Act, Pub. L. No. 103-3, 139 Cong. Rec. 1993.

Families and Work Institute (2002). *A new generation at work.* An issue brief. American Business Collaboration.

Fried, M. (1998). *Taking time: Parental leave policy and corporate culture.* Philadelphia: Temple University Press.

Galinsky, E. (1994). Families and work: The importance of the quality of the work environment. In S.L. Kagan & B. Weissbound (Eds.), *Putting families first.* San Francisco: Jossey-Bass.

Galinsky, E., Bond, J.T., & Friedman, D.E. (1993). *The changing workforce: Highlights of the National Study.* New York: Families and Work Institute.

Galinsky, E., Bond, J.T., & Hill, E.J. (2004). *When work works: A status report on workplace flexibility.* New York: Families and Work Institute.

Galinsky, E., Bond, J.T., & Swanberg, J. (1998). *The 1997 Study of the Changing Work force.* New York: Families and Work Institute.

Galinsky, E., Friedman, D.E., & Hernandez, C.A. (1991). *The corporate reference guide to work family programs.* New York: Families and Work Institute.

Generation and gender in the workplace (2004). New York: Families and Work Institute.

Gerson, K. (1998). Gender and the future of the family: Implications for the postin-dustrial workplace. In D. Vannoy & P. Dubeck (Eds.), *Challenges for work and family in the twenty-first century.* New York: Aldine de Gruyter.

Gerstel, N., & McGonagle, K. (1999). Job leaves and the limits of the Family and Medical Leave Act: The effects of gender, race, and family. *Work and Occupations, 26,* 510–534.

Gide, A. (1927). *The counterfeiters: A novel.* New York: Alfred A. Knopf, Inc.

Glass, J., & Camarigg, V. (1992). Gender, parenthood, and job-family compatibility. *American Journal of Sociology, 98,* 131–151.

Glass, J., & Estes, S.B. (1997). The family responsive workplace. *Annual Review of Sociology, 23,* 289–314.

Glass, J., & Riley, L. (1998). Family responsive policies and employee retention fol-lowing childbirth. *Social Forces, 76,* 1401–1435.

Golden, L. (2001). Flexible work schedules: Which workers get them? *American Behavioral Scientist, 44,* 1157–1178.

Gornick, J., & Meyers, M. (2003). *Families that work: Policies for reconciling parenthood and employment.* New York: Russell Sage Foundation.

Grover, S.L. (1991). Predicting the perceived fairness of parental leave policies. *Jour-nal of Applied Psychology, 76,* 247–255.

Harris Interactive YouthPulse (2003). Rochester, NY, http://www.harrisinteractive .com/news/allnewsbydate.asp?NewsID=667.

Hochschild, A.R. (1987). *The second shift.* New York: Viking Penguin.

Hochschild, A.R. (1997). *The time bind: When work becomes home and home becomes work.* New York: Metropolitan Books.

Howe, N., & Strauss, W. (2000). *Millennials rising: The next great generation.* New York: Vintage Books.

Hyde, J.S., Essex, M.J., Clark, R., Klein, M.H., & Byrd, J. (1996). Parental leave: Policy and research. *Journal of Social Issues, 52,* 91–109.

Jacobs, J., & Gerson, K. (2001). Overworked individuals or overworked families: Explaining trends in work, leisure and family time. *Work and Occupations, 28,* 40–63.

Jacobs, J., & Gerson, K. (2004a). *The time divide: Balancing work and family in contempo-rary society.* Cambridge, MA: Harvard University Press.

Jacobs, J., & Gerson, K. (2004b). *The time divide: Work, family and gender inequality.* Cambridge, MA: Harvard University Press.

Jacobs, J., & Gerson, K. (2004c). The work-home crunch. *Contexts, 3,* 29–37.

Judiesch, M.K., & Lyness, K.S. (1999). Left behind? The impact of leaves of absence on managers' career success. *Academy of Management Journal, 42,* 641–651.

Kemp, A.A. (1994). *Women's work: Degraded and devalued.* Englewood Cliffs, NJ: Prentice Hall.

Kunz Center for the Study of Work and Family (1998). *Ohio wives still stuck with most of the housework, finds statewide survey by University of Cincinnati.* http:// asweb.artsci.uc.edu/sociology/kunzctr/jun398.htm.

Matthaei, J.A. (1982). *An economic history of women in America: Women's work, the sexual division of labor and the development of capitalism.* New York: Schocken Brooks.

Menaghan, E.G. (1991). Work, experiences and family interaction processes: The long reach of the job? *Annual Review of Sociology, 17,* 419–444.

Menaghan, E.G., & Parcel, T.L. (1991). Determining children's home environments: The impact of maternal characteristics and current occupational and family conditions. *Journal of Marriage and Family*, *53*, 417–431.

Pleck, J. (1993). Are family-supportive employer policies relevant to men? In J. Hood, (Ed.), *Men, work, and family*. Newbury Park, CA: Sage Publications.

Powell, G.N., & Mainiero, L.A. (1999). Managerial decision making regarding alternative work arrangements. *Journal of Occupational and Organizational Psychology*, *72*, 41–51.

Schopenhauer, A. (1928). On women. In W.H. Parker (Ed.), *Schopenhauer selections*. New York: Charles Scribner's Sons.

Schwartz, F.N. (1989). Management women and the new facts of life. *Harvard Business Review*, 65–76.

Smith, J.W., & Clurman, A. (1997). *Rocking the ages: The Yankelovich Report on generational marketing*. New York: Harper Business.

Sterling, D. (1996). Women's work and protective legislation. In P. Dubeck & K. Borman (Eds.), *Women and work: A handbook*. New York: Garland.

Strauss, W., & Howe, N. (1991). *Generations: The history of America's future*, 1584–2069. New York: Quill.

Thompson, C., Beauvais, L., & Lyness, K. (1999). When work-family benefits are not enough: The influence of work-family culture on benefit utilization, organizational attachment and work-family conflict. *Journal of Vocational Behavior*, *54*, 392–415.

U.S. Census. (2001). *Statistical Abstract of the United States 2000*. U.S. Department of Commerce. www.census.gov/prod/www/statistical-abstract.html.

U.S. Census. (2002). *Statistical Abstract of the United States 2001*. U.S. Department of Commerce. www.census.gov/prod/www/statistical-abstract.html.

U.S. Census. (2005). *Statistical Abstract of the United States*. 2004–2005. U.S. Department of Commerce. www.census.gov/prod/www/statistical-abstract.html.

U.S. Census Bureau. (2004–2005). *Statistical Abstract of the United States*. Washington, DC.

U.S. Department of Labor (2000). *20 Facts on Women Workers*. Women's Bureau. http://www.dol.gov/wb.

U.S. Department of Labor (2003). *Women in the Labor Force*. Quick Facts. Women's Bureau. http://www.dol.gov/wb.

Waldfogel, J. (1997). Working mothers then and now: A cross-cohort analysis of the effects of maternity leave on women's pay. In F. Blau & R. Ehrenberg (Eds.), *Gender and family issues in the workplace*. New York: Russell Sage.

Wayne, J.H., & Cordeiro, B.L. (2003). Who is a good organizational citizen? Social perceptions of male and female employees who use family leave. *Sex Roles*, *49*, 233–246.

Yorburg, B. (1987). Sexual identity in human history. In J. Stimson & A. Stimson (Eds.), *Sociology: Contemporary readings*. Itasca, IL: F.E. Peacock Publishers.

CHAPTER 2

Work/Life Integration: Impact on Women's Careers, Employment, and Family

Michele A. Paludi, Rebecca Vaccariello, Traci Graham,
Melissa Smith, Kelsey Allen-Dicker, Hilary Kasprzak, and
Christa White

These days, a company may see a work-family policy as a frill it can't afford. But these policies are absolutely essential, given that most people today have responsibilities at home as well as work.

—Ann Bookman, Director of MIT Workplace Center

Working outside the home is not progress if women must also continue with full-time responsibility for housekeeping and motherhood, performing "double duty" or the "second shift."

—Arlie Hochschild

Jean Stone was President and Chief Executive Officer of Dukane Corporation. She described herself as highly achievement oriented and has an intense focus on her job. She has admitted to losing sight of her personal life. Divorced after a ten-year marriage, she acknowledged that "career and work pressures were a factor in that." Debra Fields, founder of Mrs. Fields Cookies, reported starting her business because it would give her the flexibility to balance her child-rearing duties with work. Diane Graham is employed at Stratco. She gave birth to four babies, all of whom she has brought to the office as infants. In addition, she took her babies on business trips with her for the first four to five months of their lives.

What is the right balance between work and personal life? How much would women be willing to give up to be a chief executive officer of a major company? And, as a chief executive officer, what ethical responsibilities, if any, do women have to assist their employees in balancing their work and personal lives?

In this chapter we review the impact of employed mothers on children's achievement and social development, legislation to ease the integration of family and work roles (i.e., Family and Medical Leave Act), child care and elder care, and family-friendly policies to assist employees in integrating work and family roles.

Impact of Maternal Employment on Children

Maternal employment has increased dramatically in the past 25 years (Hill, Waldfogel, Brooks-Gunn, & Han, 2005; Rosenthal & Hansen, 1981; Strassel, Colgan, & Goodman, 2006). Women with infants have had the fastest growth in labor-force participation of all groups in the United States (Committee on Ways and Means, 1988; Han, Walfogel, & Brooks-Gunn, 2001). Women are now as likely to be employed when they have infants as they are when they have an older preschool-aged child. Furthermore, of women who put in overtime work, 40 percent have children under six years of age (Strassel, et al., 2006).

Maternal employment has been found to be related to positive impacts on children (Betz, in press; Beyer, 1995; Fulgini & Brooks-Gunn, 2000; Han, Waldfogel, & Brooks-Gunn, 2001; Hoffman & Youngblade, 1999; Huston & Rosenkrantz, 2005). For example, daughters of employed mothers are more career oriented (versus home oriented) than daughters of full-time homemakers. In addition, daughters of employed mothers are also more willing to pursue nontraditional careers than daughters of full-time homemakers. Betz (1993, in press) reported that girls socialized by two employed parents were more likely to combine lifestyle and work roles than girls not reared in such families. Thus, maternal employment influences women's career development through its provision of a role model of women's employment and integration of roles (Gottfried, Gottfried, & Bathurst, 2002). Girls whose mothers are employed have less restricted views of gender roles.

Hoffman and Youngblade (1999) reported that employed mothers place considerable emphasis on independence training. In addition, research with ethnic minority individuals has consistently demonstrated that maternal employment is positively associated with academic achievement (Burchinal, Roberts, Nabors, & Bryant, 1996; Clark-Stewart, 1993).

Beyer (1995) and Huston and Rosenkrantz (2005) reported that rather than employment itself and the time spent away from children, it is the mothers' personalities, beliefs, and circumstances that influence the quality of their parenting. Huston and Rosenkrantz's study considered the impact of maternal employment on infants' development. Huston and Rosenkrantz reported that employed mothers compensate for time away from home. For example, they spent more time with their children on their days off from work and less time on household tasks, leisure, and other activities. Wille (1992) found that mothers who were less satisfied with their roles (e.g., they had to return to work because of economic reasons) were less autonomous and more anxious on reunion with their infants each day. Thus, in addition to benefiting children, maternal employment usually benefits mothers themselves. Research indicates that maternal employment is a boost to the morale of mothers and a buffer against anxieties (Hoffman & Youngblade, 1999; Raver, 2003). Etaugh and Nekolny (1988) suggested that one stressor for employed mothers is the perceptions people hold about mothers who work outside the home in addition to caring for their children. Etaugh and Nekolny reported that employed mothers (especially married women) were perceived as more professionally competent than nonemployed mothers. However, employed mothers were perceived as less dedicated to their families and less sensitive to the needs of others than nonemployed mothers. Married women were viewed as better adjusted than unmarried women.

Thus, maternal employment per se may have little impact on the mother-infant relationship. However, other factors associated with maternal employment (e.g., mother's role satisfaction; others' perceptions) may have more consistent influence on mother-infant relationships. In addition, factors that increase the mother's satisfaction with her multiple roles are the availability of quality child care and involvement of the child's father in child care. Both of these factors in turn promote a successful mother-child relationship (Lerner & Galambos, 1986; Weinraub, Jaeger, & Hoffman, 1988).

Maternal Employment and Child Care

One complement to maternal employment is the nature and quality of child care received (Anme & Segal, 2003; Caruso, 1996; Maccoby & Lewis, 2003). More children between the ages of birth and two years are being placed in nonparental care during the workday than ever in U.S. history (Maccoby & Lewis, 2003) as a consequence of maternal employment. Child care is defined as nonparental care in a child's own home, another's home, or in a child care center that provides children with learning opportunities that supplement and/or complement opportunities provided in the child's home.

Research has indicated that children's emotional, cognitive, and social development is less dependent on the form of child care than on the quality of such care (Shonkoff & Phillips, 2000). When children are in high-quality child care, there is no negative impact on their interpersonal relationships with their mothers, other adults, or peers or on their emotional adjustment (Boschee & Jacobs, 1997; Caruso, 1996; Hill, et al., 2005). Quality child care has been defined by the American Public Health Association and the American Academy of Pediatrics as follows:

Child-staff ratios of three to one for children under 25 months, four to one for children 25 to 30 months and seven to one for children 31 to 35 months,
Group sizes of six for children under 25 months, eight for children 25 to 30 months and 14 for children 31 to 35 months,
Child-care providers who have formal, post-high-school training in child development, early childhood education or a related field for all child-care workers at all ages.

In addition, Boschee and Jacobs (1997) reported that positive child care providers have a warm, caring, and gentle disposition and are cognizant of cultural similarities and distinctiveness among children. Boschee and Jacobs (1997) further recommended that one important aspect to quality child care is a variety of toys with which children can play. These toys must be developmentally appropriate for children of various ages and stages of cognitive development (Bornstein, Haynes, Pascual, Painter, & Galperin, 1999).

Tran and Weinraub (2006) reported that quality child care was related to advantages in language and socioemotional outcomes. Failure to meet these standards of quality child care undermines children's emotional, social, and cognitive development (Burchinal, et al., 1996; Phillips, Voran, Kisker, Howes, & Whitebook, 1994).

Paternal Involvement in Child Care and Child Development

Paternal involvement in child rearing is significantly related to later positive child outcomes (Flouri & Buchanan, 2002; Halpern, 2005). However, researchers have noted that fathers assume relatively little responsibility for child-related tasks (Flouri & Buchanan, 2002). Several variables have been found to be related to paternal involvement, including father's age, children's sex, and mother's work status (Volling & Belsky, 1991). Fathers in their late 20s or early 30s at the birth of their first child are typically more responsive, affectionate, and stimulating with their infants as well as more involved in the care of their preschool children (Volling & Belsky, 1991).

In addition, fathers have been found to be more involved with their sons' care than with their daughters' care. Fathers of boys are also more likely to spend time with their sons in play, project activities, and private talks than with their daughters (Marsiglio, 1991).

DeLuccie (1996) and Parke and Swain (1980) reported that maternal employment is a significant predictor of fathers' interaction time with their children. Fathers in families where mothers worked outside the home were more engaged, accessible, and responsible for child care tasks than fathers who were the sole financial support for the families. However, McBride and Mills (1993) caution that these data may be a result of employed mothers doing less, not because of fathers doing more with children.

Fathers play an important role in girls' career choices (Cabrera, Tamis-LeMonda, Bradley, Hofferth, & Lamb, 2000; Lamb, 1997). Fathers' support is especially important when girls are pursuing nontraditional careers rather than traditional careers.

Employed Women and Elder Care

Many women are postponing childbearing until their late 30s and early 40s (Lockwood, 2003). By the time these women begin their families, their parents are aged 60 years or older. Thus, in addition to caring for young children, many employed women in the United States are also caring for elderly parents, referred to as the "in-between" or "sandwiched" generation (Halpern, 2005; Hammer, Neal, Newsom, Brockwood, & Colton, 2005; Lockwood, 2003). Forty percent of women caring for elders also have child care responsibilities. It has been estimated that women spend seventeen years of their lives caring for children and eighteen years caring for one or both parents (Lockwood, 2003).

By the year 2030, one of five citizens in the United States will be above 65 years of age (Dreifus, 2006). The requirement for caregiving progressively ascends after age 65; at age 85 and older, more than half of elderly individuals cannot function without caregiving. Because Medicare does not cover long-term care for the elderly, new forms of long-term aid must be developed (Dreifus, 2006). Currently, the primary caregiver is the family, most likely the elderly individual's daughter or daughter-in-law (Abel, 1991; Brody, 1990; Hammer, et al., 2005; Remennick, 1999). Since women live, on the average, five to seven years longer than men, they form the majority among caregivers (as well as recipients of care) (Remennick, 1999). The National Alliance for Caregiving and the American Association of Retired Persons noted that between 44 to 61 percent of adult daughters who assume the caregiving role of elderly parents are also employed full or part time (Moen, Robison, & Fields, 1994).

Impact of Juggling Multiple Roles on Women

There are noted costs to women who integrate work and family. The importance women place on relationships may contribute to stress-related illnesses (Bainbridge, Cregan, & Kulik, 2006; Karsten, 2006). Employed women who report experiencing work/life conflict are as much as thirty times more likely to experience a significant mental health problem, e.g., depression or anxiety, than women employees who report no work/life conflict (Gonzalez-Morales, Peiro, & Greenglass, 2006). Because women are integrating work and child and elder care, they work longer than men. Longer work hours impact emotional and physical well-being (Karsten, 2006).

Research has identified psychological symptoms associated with integrating work and life (Karsten, 2006; Lundberg-Love, in press). These symptoms include, but are not limited to:

Fear	Anger	Isolation
Guilt	Shame	Panic Reactions
Anxiety	Phobias	Self-consciousness
Helplessness	Frustration	Insecurity
Shock	Confusion	Fear of new people
Depression	Alienation	Withdrawal from work and
Decreased self-esteem	Denial	from social situations

Research has also documented a variety of physical health complaints among women integrating multiple roles. These symptoms include, but are not limited to:

Headaches	Tiredness	Inability to Concentrate
Eating Disorders	Lethargy	Gastrointestinal Disorders
Dermatological Problems	Respiratory Problems	

Organizational responses to stress include:

Increased Turnover	Workplace Accidents	Workplace Violence

Common behavioral symptoms include:

Impaired Decision Making	Sleep Disorders	Alcohol and Other Drug Abuse

Heyman (2000) noted that there is an impact on children's health when parents are not achieving work/life balance. For example, she reported the following:

— Sick children have shorter recovery periods, better vital signs, and fewer symptoms when their parents participate in their care.
— The presence of a parent reduces hospital stays by 31 percent. When parents are involved in children's care, children recover more rapidly from outpatient procedures.
— Parents play important roles in the care of children with chronic as well as acute conditions. Receiving care from their parents is important for children's mental as well as physical health.
— There is a significant impact on children's educational outcomes when parents are not achieving work/life balance. When parents are involved in their children's education, children achieve more at all grade levels.
— Parental involvement is associated with children's higher achievement in language and mathematics, improved behavior, greater academic persistence, and lower dropout rates.

Hewlett and Luce (2006) noted that women indicated their children experienced the following due to the number of hours they worked each week: watching too much television, acting out/lack of attention, eating too much junk food, and having too little adult supervision and underachieving in school. Hewlett and Luce offered the comments from one participant in their research:

> When I walk out the door in the morning, leaving my two-year-old with the nanny, there's usually a bit of a scene. Tommy clings, pouts, and whips up the guilt. Now, I know it's not serious...he's a happy kid, and he likes his nanny. But it sure makes me think about why I go to work and why I put in a ten-hour day. It's as though every day I make this calculation: Do the satisfactions I derive from my job (efficacy, recognition, a sense of stretching my mind) justify leaving Tommy? Some days it's a close run.

Hewlett and Luce (2006) also noted that 57 percent of the women in their survey told them they do not want to continue working long days for more than a year. Eighty percent of the women in global companies indicated they did not want to keep working long hours for more than a year. Hewlett and Luce interpreted these results as indicating women are more in tune than men to the "fallout on their children...they see a direct link between their long workweeks and a variety of distressing behaviors in their children" (p. 56).

Furthermore, stress is additive. Each new stressor adds to an employee's stress level. One single stressor may be relatively unimportant in and of itself. However, if it is added to an already high level of stress, it can be too devastating for the woman. Time pressures are not the primary cause of work/life conflicts. Rather, it is the psychological inclusion of family life into the work domain and, conversely, work into the family domain. Employees are worrying about their family and/or personal problems at work and thinking about their work-related problems at home (Ezzedeen & Swiercz, 2002). Ezzedeen and Swiercz found that this cognitive intrusion of work results in lower job satisfaction, a greater incidence of work/life conflict, job burnout, and less overall happiness. They also reported that the experience of intrusion is rooted in the organizational culture of the employer, including whether or not the employer has family-friendly policies (to be discussed later in this chapter).

Strategies to assist employees in dealing with the stress involved in integrating work and family lives offered by Paludi and Paludi (2006) include time management techniques, increasing physical exercise, relaxation training, and increasing social support networks.

Federal Responses

The Family and Medical Leave Act of 1993 (FMLA) was enacted with the stated purposes of helping employees balance the demands of work and family life; entitling employees to take reasonable leave for their own medical reasons, for the birth or adoption of a child, or the care of a child, spouse, or parent with a serious medical condition; and accommodating the legitimate interests of employers, while also allowing employees equal employment opportunity by offering gender-neutral medical leave options.

FMLA applies to all employees working for public employers and to employees of private employers of fifty or more employees. An employee is eligible for FMLA once he or she has worked for an employer for one year, and he or she must have been employed at least 1,250 hours in the year prior to the FMLA leave. FMLA allows an employee to take up to twelve work-weeks of unpaid leave in a twelve-month period for multiple family medical purposes. FMLA may be taken intermittently, and the employee may also work a reduced schedule if medically necessary to care for a family member or the employee's own serious health condition, defined under FMLA as illnesses or physical or mental conditions that involve a period of incapacity resulting from inpatient medical care, continuing medical treatment, pregnancy, or treatment for a chronic serious health condition (e.g., stroke, Alzheimer's disease, diabetes, asthma, epilepsy, and cancer).

Employers may require employees to use their paid leave accruals for some or all of their FMLA leave. In addition, an employer is required to maintain employees' group health insurance coverage during their FMLA leave. When an employee returns from FMLA leave, the employer must restore the employee to his or her original job or an equivalent job in terms of pay, benefits, and other employment terms.

The overall effect of FMLA has been to increase the family leave taken by employees (Gale, 2006; Waldfogel, 1999). While family leave use has increased among both employees who were covered under FMLA and those who were not, the largest increase in family leave use has been seen in employees who are covered by FMLA (Waldfogel, 1999).

Furthermore, maternity and paternity leaves have shown an increase by covered employees since the passage of FMLA; paternity leave has shown a sharper increase (Gale, 2006; Waldfogel, 1999). FMLA has had a significant impact on family leave use (Waldfogel, 1999). Research has suggested that FMLA has not had an effect on productivity or profitability in the workplace (Waldfogel, 1999).

Reasons for employees taking FMLA have changed since 1995. There are currently more employees taking leave for maternity leave and leave to care for a sick parent or spouse (Society for Human Resource Management [SHRM], 2003; Waldfogel, 2001). However, critics of FMLA have noted that this legislation is not "family friendly" at all (see Dziech, chapter 1, this volume). Golden (2001), for example, found that employees tend to refuse FMLA because they are concerned with job mobility. Wayne and Cordeiro (2003) noted that men who take FMLA are perceived negatively by co-workers due to stereotypes about men and caregiving (Deaux & Kite, 1993; Doyle & Paludi, 1997).

We note that in 1997 then United States Senator John D. Ashcroft introduced "The Family Friendly Workplace Act," which specifically cited the need for employers to provide more flexible work schedules. As Strassel, et al. (2006) noted,

The act would have given companies and their employees three options: a biweekly work schedule that allowed employees to work 80 hours over two weeks in any hourly combination; compensatory time-and-a half off…or flexible credit hours that would allow workers to save up labor past 40 hours one week toward paid leave later on. (p. 28)

This Act met with opposition from labor unions that suggested that this Act would abolish worker protections by eliminating the forty-hour workweek. The Act was blocked by Congress.

Employed parents are eligible for the Child and Dependent Care Tax Credit. Parents who work full time can claim from 20 to 35 percent of child care expenses for children under age 13 against their income tax liability (IRS, 2003). If there are two parents in the home, both must be employed in order to be eligible for this tax credit. Parents are also eligible for the Child Tax Credit if they are employed or not employed. However, these tax credits are small relative to the actual costs of child and elder care.

Organizational Responses

The research findings summarized in this chapter highlight the necessity for women to have greater flexibility at work as well as assistance with family responsibilities. Eighty-one percent of women would select a job with more flexibility and benefits over a job that offers a higher salary (Center for Policy Alternatives Women's Program, 2000). Companies that recognize the need and adapt work to employees' lives will win employees' loyalty and thus have a competitive edge. Their challenge is to restore the balance of work and personal life. Companies have accomplished this through the following strategies: time-based, information-based, direct services and culture change policies (DeCenzo & Robbins, 2005; Hewlett & Luce, 2006; Kahnweiler & Kahnweiler, 1992; Strassel, et al., 2006). These organizations report positive ramifications for the businesses from family-oriented or family-friendly policies as well as for parents: lower absenteeism, less stress, higher morale, positive publicity, improved work satisfaction, lower turnover rate, staffing over a wide range of hours, child care hours that conform to work hours, and access to quality infant and child care (Frone & Yardley, 1996).

Time-based strategies include flextime, job sharing, part-time work, and telecommuting (Brewer, 2000; see Cioffi, chapter 6, this volume; DeCenzo & Robbins, 2005; Golden, 2001; Kossek, Barber, & Winters, 1999). For example, Mentor Graphics Corporation has 98 percent of its employees using flextime, a policy that allows employees to set their own hours and schedules within limits set by their employer. Employees at IBM receive three years of job-guaranteed leave following childbirth. TriHealth in Cincinnati, Ohio, offers flextime, telecommuting, job sharing, and compressed workweeks. A minimum of sixteen hours per week must be spent working in order to receive health benefits. In addition, TriHealth provides an on-site child care center, trained nurses who are available to care for sick children at the homes of the employees for two dollars per day, and a on-site gym and play place for children.

American Express provides flextime for employees. Lehman Brothers provides networks of employees and mentors and flexibility for women who take time off from work for child care and eldercare responsibilities and later want to return to work.

Information-based strategies include programs/policies such as intranet work, relocation assistance, and eldercare resources. At Ernst & Young, for example, employees are provided with intranet sites that include information on how to write flexible work arrangement proposals.

Direct services include policies/programs such as on-site child care, emergency backup care, and on-site health services. S.C. Johnson offers employees subsidized concierge services for car maintenance, and a grocery shopping service. AFLAC provides on-site child care centers. At Stratus Technologies, on-site mammograms and skin cancer testing are provided. At Johnson & Johnson, "nurture spaces" are provided that allow quiet, comfortable facilities with trained professional counselors to help new mothers succeed at breastfeeding while returning to work. AFLAC offers two on-site child care centers at its headquarters in Columbus, Georgia. This is the largest corporate child care site in Georgia. Educational programs, including study in math and science, are also offered. Employees at AFLAC's Albany and Omaha sites are provided child care subsidies. The JFK Medical Center in Florida offers an on-site child care center as well as a workplace-based charter school, where before and after school, holiday, summer, and hurricane-emergency care are provided. Protective Life Insurance Company in Birmingham, Alabama, offers sick-child day care as a component of its health and wellness benefits.

While not as common as on-site child care facilities, some companies are offering work/life programs that address eldercare (SHRM, 2003). These programs include paid eldercare, emergency eldercare, subsidy of eldercare cost, and eldercare referral services.

Culture change strategies include programs that provide training for managers to help deal with work/life conflicts. In addition, placing focus on employees' actual performance and not "face time" at the job is another culture change strategy. Lucent, Marriott, Merck, Prudential, and Xerox all link managers' pay to employees' satisfaction with their supervisory performance.

Work/Life Planning

A new approach to helping women and men deal with integrating work and family has been identified as total life planning (Lockwood, 2003). The goal of this program is to assist employees in doing "developmental work" (Lewis & Butler, 1974), i.e., to recall and examine past experiences to help them resolve, reorganize, and reintegrate their concerns. Employees are encouraged to do a "life review," i.e., to look at their lives as not being composed

of separate spheres of work and life but rather as a whole and to assess relationships, emotional health, physical well-being, careers, religiosity, financial
situation, and parenting skills. Employees learn how to develop an individualized life plan, to "set a goal-oriented environment with a meaningful and
transformational component for each individual" (Traynor, 1999, p. 30).

Lockwood (2003) and Martinez (1997) reported that total life planning is
related to increased employee energy, enthusiasm for work, and increased
productivity. Total life planning requires discussions with employees that
deal with private issues that typically have not been brought into the workplace (e.g., lesbian and gay relationships, divorce, bankruptcy, and addic-
tions). Well-trained human resource specialists and/or employee assistance
programs can assist in this regard.

Miller (2005) noted that the work/life programs rated highest by human resource specialists for reducing unscheduled absences are as follows:

1. Alternative work arrangements,
2. Flu shot programs,
3. Leave for school functions,
4. Telecommuting,
5. Compressed workweek,
6. On-site child care,
7. Emergency child care,
8. Employee assistance programs,
9. Wellness programs,
10. On-site health services,
11. Fitness facility,
12. Satellite workplaces,
13. Job sharing, and
14. Eldercare services.

Miller (2005) also noted that the top work/life programs utilized by
employees in the United States companies are the following:

1. Employee assistance plans,
2. Leave for school functions,
3. Wellness programs,
4. Flu shot programs, and
5. Fitness facilities.

Lockwood (2003) noted,

Work/life programs have the potential to significantly improve employee
morale, reduce absenteeism, and retain organizational knowledge, particularly

during difficult economic times. In today's global marketplace, as companies aim to reduce costs, it falls to the human resource professional to understand the critical issues of work/life balance and champion work/life programs. Be it employees whose family members and/or friends are called to serve their country, single mothers who are trying to raise their children and make a living, Generation X and Y employees who value their personal time, couples struggling to manage dual-career marriages, or companies losing critical knowledge when employees leave for other opportunities, work/life programs offer a win-win situation for employers and employees.

We recommend the following for employers who are establishing work/life programs for their employees:

1. Revise policies and procedures to ensure they are family friendly and not discriminatory toward men and/or women;
2. Facilitate training programs for managers to ensure they understand the family-friendly policies initiated by the organization;
3. Communicate family-friendly policies via company newsletters, bulletin boards, employee handbooks, company-wide meetings, intranet, and e-mails;
4. Using anonymous surveys and/or focus groups, ask employees for their opinions on ways the organization is assisting them in integrating work and life issues.

Additional resources for employers and employees are presented in Chapter 8.

Acknowledgment

We thank Carmen A. Paludi, Jr., for comments on earlier drafts of this chapter.

References

Abel, E. (1991). *Who cares for the elderly? Public policy and the experiences of adult daughters.* Philadelphia: Temple University Press.

Anme, T., & Segal, U. (2003). Center-based evening child care: Implications for young children's development. *Early Childhood Education Journal, 30,* 137–143.

Bainbridge, H., Cregan, C., & Kulik, C. (2006). The effect of multiple roles on caregiver stress outcomes. *Journal of Applied Psychology, 91,* 490–497.

Betz, N. (1993). Career development. In F. Denmark & M. Paludi (Eds.), *Psychology of women: A handbook of issues and theories.* Westport, CT: Praeger.

Betz, N. (in press). Career development. In F. Denmark & M. Paludi (Eds.), *Psychology of women: A handbook of issues and theories. 2nd ed.* Westport, CT: Praeger.

Beyer, S. (1995). Maternal employment and children's academic achievement: Parenting styles as mediating variable. *Developmental Review, 15,* 212–253.

Bornstein, M., Haynes, O., Pascual, L., Painter, K., & Galperin, C. (1999). Play in two societies: Pervasiveness of process, specificity of structure. *Child Development, 70,* 317–331.

Boschee, M., & Jacobs, G. (1997). *Ingredients for quality child care*. New York: National Network for Child Care.

Brewer, A. (2000). Work design for flexible work scheduling: Barriers and gender implications. *Gender, work and organization, 7*, 33–44.

Brody, E. (1990). *Women in the middle: Their parent-care years*. New York: Springer.

Burchinal, M., Roberts, J., Nabors, L., & Bryant, D. (1996). Quality of center child care and infant cognitive and language development. *Child Development, 67*, 606–620.

Cabrera, N., Tamis-LeMonda, C., Bradley, R., Hofferth, S., & Lamb, M. (2000). Fatherhood in the twenty-first century. *Child Development, 71*, 127–136.

Caruso, D. (1996). Maternal employment status, mother-infant interaction, and infant development. *Child and Youth Care Forum, 25*, 125–134.

Center for Policy Alternatives Women's Program (2000). *Women's voices 2000. Key Findings*.

Clark-Stewart, A. (1993). *Daycare*. Cambridge, MA: Harvard University Press.

Committee on Ways and Means, U.S. House of Representatives (1988). *Overview of entitlement programs: 1998 Green Book*. Washington, DC: U.S. Government Printing Office.

Deaux, K., & Kite, M. (1993). Gender stereotypes. In F.L. Denmark & M. Paludi (Eds.), *Psychology of women: A handbook of issues and theories*. Westport, CT: Praeger.

DeCenzo, D., & Robbins, S. (2005). Fundamentals of human resource management. New York: Wiley.

DeLuccie, M. (1996). Predictors of paternal involvement and satisfaction. *Psychological Reports, 79*, 1351–1359.

Dempsey, K. (1999). Attempting to explain women's perceptions of the fairness of the division of housework. *Journal of Family Studies, 5*, 3–24.

Doyle, J., & Paludi, M. (1997). *Sex and gender: The human experience*. New York: McGraw-Hill.

Dreifus, C. (2006). Focusing on the issue of aging, and growing into the job. *New York Times*, November 14.

Etaugh, C., & Nekolny, K. (1998, August). *Perceptions of mothers: Effects of employment status and marital status*. Paper presented at the annual conference of the American Psychological Association, Atlanta, GA.

Ezzedeen, S., & Swiercz, P. (2002). *Rethinking worklife balance: Development and validation of the cognitive intrusion of work scale—A dissertation research proposal*. Proceedings of the 2002 Eastern Academy of Management Meeting.

Flouri, E., & Buchanan, A. (2002). What predicts fathers' involvement with their children? A prospective study of intact families. *British Journal of Developmental Psychology, 21*, 81–98.

Frone, M., & Yardley, J. (1996). Workplace family-supportive programmes: Predictors of employed parents' importance ratings. *Journal of Occupational and Organizational Psychology, 69*, 351–366.

Fulgini, A., & Brooks-Gunn, J. (2000). *The healthy development of young children: SES disparities, prevention studies, and policy opportunities*. Washington, DC: National Academy of Sciences.

Gale, J. (2006). The Family and Medical Leave Act: Lost in translation. In M. Karsten (Ed.), *Gender, race, and ethnicity in the workplace*, pp. 119–141. Westport, CT: Praeger.

Golden, L. (2001). Flexible work schedules: Which workers get them? *American Behavioral Scientist, 44*, 1157–1158.

Gonzalez-Morales, M., Peiro, J., & Greenglass, E. (2006). Coping and distress in organizations: The role of gender in work stress. *International Journal of Stress Management, 13*, 228–248.

Gottfried, A., Gottfried, A., & Bathurst, K. (2002). Maternal and dual-earner employment status and parenting. In M. Borstein (Ed.), *Handbook of parenting. 2nd ed.* Mahwah, NJ: Erlbaum.

Halpern, D. (2005). Psychology at the intersection of work and family: Recommendations for employers, working families, and policymakers. *American Psychologist, 60*, 397–409.

Hammer, L., Neal, M., Newsom, J., Brockwood, K., & Colton, C. (2005). A longitudinal study of the effects of dual-earner couples' utilization of family workplace supports on work and family outcomes. *Journal of Applied Psychology, 90*, 799–810.

Han, W., Waldfogel, J., & Brooks-Gunn, J. (2001). The effects of early maternal employment on later cognitive and behavioral outcomes. *Journal of Marriage and the Family, 63*, 336–354.

Hewlett, S., & Luce, C. (2006). Extreme jobs: The dangerous allure of the 70-hour workweek. *Harvard Business Review*, December, 49–59.

Heyman, J. (Ed.) (2000). *The widening gap: Why American working families are in jeopardy and what can be done about it.* New York: Basic Books.

Hill, J., Waldfogel, J., Brooks-Gunn, J., & Han, E.J. (2005). Maternal employment and child development: A fresh look using newer methods. *Developmental Psychology, 41*, 833–850.

Hoffman, L., & Youngblade, L. (1999). Maternal employment, morale, and parenting style: Social class comparisons. *Journal of Applied Developmental Psychology, 19*, 389–413.

Huston, A., & Rosenkrantz, A. (2005). Mothers' time with infant and time in employment as predictors of mother-child relationships and children's early development. *Child Development, 76*, 467–482.

IRS (2003). *Child and dependent care expenses for 2003*, Publication 592.

Kahnweiler, W., & Kahnweiler, J. (1992). The work/family challenge: A key career development issue. *Journal of Career Development, 18*, 251–257.

Karsten, M. (2006). Managerial women, minorities, and stress: Causes and consequences. In M. Karsten (Ed.), *Gender, race and ethnicity in the workplace*, pp. 238–272, Westport, CT: Praeger.

Kossek, E., Barber, A., & Winters, D. (1999). Using flexible schedules in the managerial world: The power of peers. *Human Resource Management, 38*, 33–46.

Lamb, M. (Ed.). (1997). *The role of the father in child development.* New York: Wiley.

Lerner, J., & Galambos, N. (1986). Child development and family change: The influences of maternal employment on infants and toddlers. *Advances in Infancy Research, 4*, 3986.

Lewis, M.I., & Butler, R.N. (1974). Life review therapy: Putting memories to work in individual and group psychotherapy. *Geriatrics, 29*, 165–169, 172–173.

Lockwood, N. (2003). Work/life balance: Challenges and solutions. *Society for Human Resource Management Research Quarterly*, June.

Lundberg-Love, P. (in press). Stress and health. In M. Paludi (Ed.), *The psychology of women at work*. Westport, CT: Praeger.

Maccoby, E., & Lewis, C. (2003). Less day care or different day care? *Child Development, 74,* 1069–1075.

Marsiglio, W. (1991). Paternal engagement activities with minor children. *Journal of Marriage and the Family, 53,* 973–986.

Martinez, M. (1997). *Work-life programs reap business benefits.* Society for Human Resource Management, June 1997.

McBride, B., & Mills, G. (1993). A comparison of mother and father involvement with their preschool age children. *Early Childhood Research Quarterly, 8,* 457–477.

Miller, S. (2005). *Work/life programs tackle unscheduled absenteeism; Improve the bottom line.* Society for Human Resource Management, October.

Moen, P., Robison, J., & Fields, K. (1994). Women's work and caregiving roles: A life course approach. *Journal of Health and Social Behavior, 36,* 259–273.

NICHD Early Child Care Research Network (2006). Child-care effect sizes for the NICHD study of early child care and youth development. *American Psychologist, 61,* 99–116.

Paludi, M., & Paludi, C. (2006, October). *Creative tools for transforming change.* Presentation for the New York State Work-Life Services, Albany, NY.

Parke, R.D., & Swain, D.B. (1980). The family in early infancy: Social interactional and attitudinal analyses. In F.A. Pedersen (Ed.), *The father-infant relationship: Observational studies in the family setting.* New York: Praeger.

Phillips, D., Voran, M., Kisker, E., Howes, C., & Whitebook, M. (1994). Child care for children in poverty: Opportunity or inequity? *Child Development, 65,* 472–492.

Raver, C. (2003). Does work pay psychologically as well as economically? The role of employment in predicting depressive symptoms and parenting among low-income families. *Child Development, 74,* 1720–1736.

Remennick, L. (1999). Women of the "sandwich" generation and multiple roles: The case of Russian immigrants of the 1990s in Israel. *Sex Roles, 32,* 347–378.

Rosenthal, D., & Hansen, J. (1981). The impact of maternal employment on children's perceptions of parents and personal development. *Sex Roles, 7,* 593–598.

Shonkoff, J., & Phillips, D. (Eds.). (2000). *From neurons to neighborhoods: The science of early childhood development.* Washington, DC: National Academy Press.

Society for Human Resource Management (2003). *SHRM 2003 benefits survey.* Alexandria, VA.

Strassel, K., Colgan, C., & Goodman, J. (2006). *Leaving women behind: Modern families, outdated laws.* New York: Rowman & Littlefield Publishers.

Tran, H., & Weinraub, M. (2006). Child care effects in context: Quality, stability and multiplicity in nonmaternal arrangements during the first 15 months of life. *Developmental Psychology, 42,* 566–582.

Traynor, J. (1999). A new frontier in work-life benefits. *Employee Benefits Journal, 24,* 29–32.

Volling, B., & Belsky, J. (1991). Multiple determinants of father involvement during infancy in dual earner and single earner families. *Journal of Marriage and the Family, 53,* 461–474.

Waldfogel, J. (1999). Family leave coverage in the 1990s. *Monthly Labor Review.* (October) 122:13–21.

Waldfogel, J. (2001). *Family and Medical Leave: Evidence from the 2000 surveys.* New York: Mimeo, Columbia University.

Wayne, J., & Cordeiro, B. (2003). Who is a good organizational citizen? Social perceptions of male and female employees who use family leave. *Sex Roles, 49*, 233–246.

Weinraub, M., Jaeger, E., & Hoffman, L. (1988). Predicting infant outcome in families of employed and non-employed mothers. *Early Childhood Research Quarterly, 3*, 361–378.

Wille, D. (1992). Maternal employment: Impact on maternal behavior. *Family Relations: Interdisciplinary Journal of Applied Family Studies, 41*, 273–277.

CHAPTER 3

Redefining the U.S. Family and Laws to Include Gay, Lesbian, Bisexual, and Transgendered Individuals: Parents and Employers in the Twenty-First Century

Eros R. DeSouza

Images of a husband and wife and their children together in a middle-class household have been infused in the psyche of U.S. society. Similarly, stereotypes of sexual minorities (e.g., lesbian, gay, bisexual, and transgender, hereafter LGBT, individuals) abound, including the stereotype that LGBT individuals are not interested in forming a family (Richman, 2002). Such images and stereotypes reflect heterosexual, white, middle-class, and individualist worldviews, which downplay or marginalize worldviews that are not heterosexual, white, middle class, and individualist. These factors interface; that is, heterosexism, racism, classism, and individualism are interrelated in any discourse about family, be it from a psychological, sociological, or legal perspective. Moreover, families of today and tomorrow will continue to challenge the traditional definition of family. According to Silverstein (2002), "gay, lesbian, and transsexual parents; single mothers by choice; and interracial adoptions and other previously labeled non-traditional families transform the societal landscape" (p. 59). These families, as well as their children (including those produced by new reproductive technologies), reflect an increasing diversity that is too complex to examine in a single chapter; hence, the current chapter will focus exclusively on LGBT individuals and their children, as well as on factors that hinder or facilitate extending universal principles of equality to include LGBT individuals.

The challenges facing LGBT individuals are many, beginning in their own families and communities of origin, which are predominantly heterosexual and may not be accepting of the sexuality of LGBT individuals. For example, in a national survey with a random sample of 405 self-identified lesbians, gay men, and bisexuals across fifteen major U.S. metropolitan areas, 34 percent of the respondents reported that at least one family member refused to accept them because of their sexual orientation (Kaiser Foundation, 2001). Social ostracism may be especially common for LGBT people of color who may feel alienated and isolated from their families and communities, and, in turn, may experience racism from society at large and oftentimes from the white lesbian and gay community (Milville & Fergunson, 2006).

Which Is Fairer: Marriage Equality or Civil Union for Same-Sex Couples?

It is often suggested that gay men are reluctant to express emotional intimacy due to the doubling of the interpersonal and expressive deficits of the male gender role socialization. Findings by Wester, Pionke, and Vogel (2005) with two samples of gay men did not support the assertion that male gender role socialization within gay men's romantic relationships compounded or doubled their reluctance to express intimacy. Two men are as capable of loving each other as are opposite-sex couples or lesbian couples. Moreover, it is decline in relationship quality, and not sexual orientation or gender per se, that predicts dissolution of a romantic relationship for gay, lesbian, and heterosexual couples (Kurdek, 2004).

It is our human nature to love and belong (e.g., Maslow, 1968). Thus, LGBT individuals have the same need for emotional intimacy (e.g., to be loved and to love) as heterosexuals. It is not surprising, then, that many LGBT individuals yearn to form families, with or without children. Despite experiencing prejudice and discrimination, the literature indicates that same-sex couples are very similar to opposite-sex couples; that is, both types of couples form stable, long-lasting, and committed relationships (e.g., Kurdek, 2004, 2005; Patterson, 2000). Patterson reported that 40 to 60 percent of gay men and 45 to 80 percent of lesbians were in committed romantic relationships. In addition, in a national survey, 74 percent of self-identified lesbians, gay men, and bisexuals reported that if they could legally marry someone of the same sex some day, they would (Kaiser Foundation, 2001). In fact, from May 17, 2004, when same-sex couples began legally marrying in Massachusetts, until February 2005, 6,142 same-sex marriages were performed in that state—35 percent were male couples and 65 percent were female couples (Adams, 2006).

Same-sex couples face an uphill battle in order to enjoy the same benefits, resources, and privileges that marriage bestows upon heterosexual couples. For example, according to the U.S. General Accounting Office (2004), as of December 31, 2003, there were 1,138 federal statutory provisions in which benefits, rights, and privileges automatically granted to married heterosexual couples could not be enjoyed by same-sex couples (e.g., Social Security survivors' benefits and the right to make medical decisions on behalf of a spouse).

In a national public opinion survey conducted in the fall of 2000 by the Kaiser Foundation (2001), 55 percent of those surveyed opposed and 39 percent supported legalizing same-sex marriage. In 2005, 36 percent of those surveyed favored allowing gays and lesbians to marry (Pew Research Center for the People and the Press, 2005). In addition, support for a U.S. Constitution ban on same-sex marriage increased to 57 percent in a Gallup Poll (2005) conducted in 2005; this is the highest increase since 2003. In 2006, the Quinnipiac University Poll (2006) reported that 24 percent of a national sample of U.S. registered voters stated that if they had to choose in their own state, they would favor allowing same-sex couples to get married. These findings suggest that the majority of the U.S. public is opposed to same-sex marriage. Moreover, forty-five states have passed laws or amendments that ban same-sex marriage; only Massachusetts allows same-sex marriage (Associated Press, 2007b).

Concerning civil unions or domestic partnerships that would give same-sex couples many of the legal rights that opposite-sex couples currently enjoy, in the fall of 2000, 47 percent of the public surveyed supported such unions and 42 percent opposed them (Kaiser Foundation, 2001). In 2005, 53 percent of those surveyed favored civil unions for gays and lesbians (Pew Research Center for the People and the Press, 2005). In 2006, the Quinnipiac University Poll (2006) reported that 44 percent of a national sample of U.S. registered voters would favor allowing same-sex couples to form civil unions. These findings suggest that the U.S. public is quite divided on this issue. Moreover, the public appears more inclined to favor same-sex civil unions than it does same-sex marriages. To date, Connecticut, Vermont, California, and most recently New Jersey offer civil unions or domestic partnerships for same-sex couples (Associated Press, 2007b).

Many in the U.S. public argue that LGBT individuals should be content with civil unions or domestic partnerships rather than marriage, because the former give same-sex couples almost the same rights as marriage does. Herek (2006) found flaws with such logic. First, marriage is accepted across all fifty states and U.S. territories, but civil unions and domestic partnerships are not. In fact, in 1996, Congress passed the "Defense of Marriage Act" in which no state is required to honor same-sex marriages performed in another state; in addition to a ban on same-sex marriage, as of November 2006, twenty-one states passed a statute and/or a constitutional amendment banning civil unions and domestic partnerships in "defense" of marriage between one man and one woman (National Gay and Lesbian Task Force, 2006). Second, almost marriage is not the same thing as marriage; thus, it is unclear whether civil unions or domestic partnerships would have the same positive psychosocial effects as marriage does (Herek, 2006). Third, Herek suggested that creating a separate, quasi-marital status for same-sex couples might stereotype them further by perpetuating and compounding the stigma associated with homosexuality. That is, civil unions or domestic partnerships might devalue and delegitimize same-sex relationships as being something less than opposite-sex relationships (see previous examples of stereotypes concerning romantic relationships between same-sex partners). Anything less than marriage equality would perpetuate power differentials and indicate that LGBT

individuals are second-class citizens without the same rights and responsibilities as heterosexuals.

In response to opponents of same-sex marriage who assert that marriage
exists for the sole purpose of procreation, supporters of same-sex marriage
recently introduced a ballot measure in the state of Washington that would
require that opposite-sex couples prove that they have had a child within
three years of their marriage; otherwise, their marriage would be annulled,
and they would be ineligible for marriage benefits just as same-sex couples
(Associated Press, 2007a). Proponents of this measure openly acknowledged
that it was "absurd," but hoped that the initiative would generate discussion
about many of the misguided assumptions on the issue of same-sex marriage.

LGBT Individuals as Parents

The previous discussion on same-sex marriage indicated a strong
opposition toward marriage equality in the United States, which might negatively affect same-sex couples and their children (Herek, 2006), especially
same-sex couples of color, many of whom are already economically disadvantaged and experiencing the double-edged sword of racial discrimination and
sexual prejudice (Dang & Frazer, 2005). Herek (2006) also pointed out
another negative consequence for a lack of marriage equality: The children
of same-sex couples do not automatically enjoy a legally defined relationship
with both parents and may be stigmatized as illegitimate or bastard by society. The sexual orientation of LGBT individuals is not the problem. Instead
prejudice toward them by society at large and other social inequalities are
the problem.

The U.S. Census counted 281.4 million people in the United States in
2000. Among people aged 15 and over, 54 percent were currently married.
Based on the total number of households (N = 105.5 million), 52 percent consisted of married couples (down from 55 percent in 1990), and 32 percent
were "nonfamily" households (an increase of 23 percent from the 1990 Census). One-person households were the second most common type of household (26 percent). Nine percent of all coupled households were unmarried
households. Same-sex unmarried-partner households represented 1 percent
of all coupled households; of these, 34 percent of female couples and 22 percent of male couples had children under 18 in the home. These findings illustrate the changing face of "family" in the contemporary United States, with
an increasing number of nontraditional households.

Based on data from the 2000 U.S. Census, Dang and Frazer (2005)
reported that there were almost 85,000 black same-sex couples, which represent about 14 percent of all same-sex couples of all races and ethnicities
(or approximately 600,000 total). Regarding parenting rates, black same-sex
couples were similar to opposite-sex black couples (married or cohabitating).
For example, black female same-sex couples were raising nonbiological children (e.g., foster or adopted) at the same rate as black married opposite-sex

couples (14 percent). Black male same-sex couples were raising nonbiological children comparable to black married opposite-sex couples (10 percent and 13 percent, respectively). In addition, black same-sex couples showed similar rates of residing in the same residence as they did five years earlier compared to black married opposite-sex couples (47 percent and 58 percent, respectively). Black same-sex couples were more likely to reside in the same residence for the past five years than were black cohabiting opposite-sex couples (47 percent and 19 percent, respectively). These findings suggest that black same-sex couples form stable families.

Opponents of LGBT individuals as parents argue that their children may be negatively affected by the sexual orientation of the parents. Although there are more studies about lesbians raising children than about gay men raising children (e.g., Peplau & Beals, 2004), and even fewer about children of transgender parents (e.g., Carter, 2006), there is a growing body of evidence that shows that children raised by lesbians, gay men, or transsexuals are, as a whole, comparable to children raised by heterosexuals (e.g., Carter, 2006; Fitzgerald, 1999; Golombok, et al., 2003; Patterson, 2004; Peplau & Beals, 2004), including evidence from longitudinal studies conducted in the United States (e.g., Gartrell, Banks, Hamilton, et al., 1999; Gartrell, Banks, Reed, et al., 2000; Gartrell, Deck, Rodas, Peyser, & Banks, 2005), as well as from a national sample of U.S. same-sex and opposite-sex families raising 12- to 18-year-old adolescents (e.g., Wainright, Russell, & Patterson, 2004). Overall, the existing evidence shows that the sexual orientation of the parents does not have a negative impact on children's or adolescents' social, emotional, and behavioral development, including their gender identity and gender-role behaviors and attitudes.

Currently, there is a baby boom for lesbians and gay men, who typically become parents through artificial insemination for lesbians, surrogate mothers for gay men, adoption, or foster care. These approaches frequently involve a lengthy, expensive, and planned process (Gartrell, et al., 1996), which suggests a deep desire and commitment by gay men and lesbians to become parents.

According to Ryan, Pearlmutter, and Groza (2004), child placement agencies should consider LGBT individuals as suitable parents for adoption and foster care; their rationale is simple: there are more children available for foster care and adoption than the number of families to take them in, especially since the number of traditional households (i.e., married opposite-sex couples) is declining. Unfortunately, a narrow definition of family that reflects sexual prejudice by child welfare workers, judges, and policy makers is hindering the placement of children in LGBT households. Downs and James (2006) studied sixty LGBT families in thirteen states and reported that the major challenges encountered by these families were discrimination by placement agencies (including insensitive, inappropriate, and difficult social workers), state or local laws that hinder successful foster parenting, failure to recognize parents' partners, and lack of support by the system to acknowledge the important role of such families, who often have to prove to be exceptional parents, to meet the needs of waiting children.

Similarly, based on interviews with ten key staff members from a social services agency and a focus group with eleven gay and lesbian adoptive and foster parents, both staff and gay and lesbian parents reported that same-sex parents have typically received greater scrutiny for adoption and foster care than have opposite-sex parents, which implies that gays and lesbians are viewed as unfit to raise adopted and foster children (Brooks & Goldberg, 2001). In addition, Brooks and Goldberg reported that gay and lesbian adoptive and foster parents were frequently placed with children with serious physical, emotional, or behavioral problems. Such a trend was also evidenced by Matthews and Cramer (2006), who stated that many of the children available for adoption or foster care by gay men and lesbians are older, part of a sibling group, or have special needs.

Many child placement agencies and gay and lesbian parents follow a "don't ask, don't tell" approach in order to avoid conflict regarding the parents' sexual orientation (Matthews & Cramer, 2006; Ryan, et al., 2004). For example, a 37-year-old white male who adopted a 21-month-old son stated,

> She [agency worker] said, "You will never be asked the question [sexual orienta-tion], and we ask that you don't give us any information that will put us in the sit-uation where we have to ask." It was done so that they [the agency] were not put in a position where they had to lie. (Matthews & Cramer, 2006, p. 328)

Such an approach may not be beneficial because it creates secrecy, confusion, and mistakes. By simply being open about the parents' sexual orientation, staff and LGBT parents are advocating equality by challenging negative stereotypes about parenting by LGBT individuals (Matthews & Cramer, 2006). It is also important to train social workers to explore their own beliefs, stereotypes, and prejudices about LGBT individuals, including attitudes about them as parents; in addition, having representatives of the LGBT community present during the adoption or foster care process seems to reduce misunderstandings and misperceptions about LGBT individuals while focusing on the best interest of the child (Ryan, et al., 2004).

Factors That Hinder or Facilitate Applying Universal Principles of Equality to LGBT Individuals

There is widespread resistance to extending universal principles of equality, justice, freedom, and dignity to LGBT individuals (Kitzinger & Wilkinson, 2004). Such resistance may be related to sexual prejudice, which Herek (2000a) defines as all negative attitudes toward a person because of his or her homosexuality. Sexually prejudiced individuals are usually male, report being exclusively heterosexual, and have limited contact with LGBT individuals; in addition, heterosexual men have a more pronounced hostility toward gay men than they do toward lesbians (e.g., Herek, 1994, 2000a, 2000b, 2002;

Seltzer, 1992). Such differences may exist because lesbians seem to pose a lesser threat to men's heterosexual hegemony than gay men do, and lesbians may be perceived as erotic by some heterosexual men. Individuals who adhere to more traditional gender roles are also more likely to have negative attitudes toward gay men and lesbians than do those with less traditional gender role orientations (e.g., Basow & Johnson, 2000; Kerns & Fine, 1994; Kilianski, 2003; McCreary, 1994; Whitley, 2001).

A brief review of research on ambivalent sexism is worthwhile because sexist attitudes seem to increase the likelihood of gender and sexual orientation discrimination (Fiske & Glick, 1995). Glick and Fiske (1996) make a distinction between two types of sexist ideologies. Benevolent sexism is a subjectively positive, but patronizing, orientation of protection, idealization, and affection toward women. Hostile sexism reflects men's violence against women and exploitation of women as sex objects. These ideologies are complementary and reinforce and justify patriarchy, including heterosexuals' hostility toward women who deviate from traditional gender roles (e.g., lesbians; Glick & Fiske, 1997). Research across six U.S. samples showed that men consistently scored significantly higher than did women on sexist ideologies; in addition, although men tended to score higher than women did on both hostile and benevolent sexism, the gender gap was larger for hostile sexism than for benevolent sexism (Glick & Fiske, 1996).

In a study across three British samples of high school students, college students, and full-time employees, Masser and Abrams (1999) found that benevolent sexism, hostile sexism, and neosexism were negatively related to support for lesbians' and gay men's rights. In addition, in a study of college students at a medium-sized midwestern U.S. public university, Whitley (2001) found that the best predictors of attitudes toward homosexuality were gender, benevolent sexism, endorsement of the traditional masculine role, and attitudes toward women. That is, being male and scoring high on these measures were associated with negative attitudes toward homosexuality.

Although seventeen states have passed laws that ban discrimination based on sexual orientation and about 100 municipalities in the other thirty-three states have passed local nondiscrimination laws (National Gay and Lesbian Task Force, 2007), it seems that it is still open season to discriminate against gay men and lesbians at the workplace with impunity from the U.S. federal courts. The Equal Employment Opportunity Commission (Equal Employment Opportunity Commission [EEOC], 2005) defines sexual harassment as a form of sex discrimination that violates Title VII of the Civil Rights Act of 1964. According to the EEOC, there are two types of sexual harassment: *quid pro quo* (e.g., sexual coercion by a superior toward a subordinate in order to obtain sexual favors) and also behavior that creates a hostile or abusive environment. Social science research has made important contributions to the understanding of sexual harassment, including same-sex sexual harassment, "without focusing on whether particular behavior would rise to the level of actionable conduct in a court of law" (Gutek & Done, 2001, p. 370).

In a recent study with U.S. and Brazilian college students on perceptions of woman-to-woman sexual harassment, DeSouza, Solberg, and Cerqueira (2007) found, overall, a significant relationship between attitudes toward lesbians and sexist ideologies. That is, respondents who scored high on hostile sexism and benevolent sexism had negative attitudes toward lesbians. In addition, respondents who had limited association with gay men and lesbians had more negative attitudes toward lesbians than respondents who frequently associated with gay men and lesbians.

Moreover, DeSouza, et al. (2007) found that—after controlling for country, gender, race/ethnicity, and sexual orientation—respondents who scored high on hostile sexism judged a hypothetical case involving two female college students as less likely to be sexual harassment and in need of an investigation, whereas respondents who scored high on perceptions of what behaviors constitute woman-to-woman sexual harassment were more likely to judge such a case as sexual harassment and in need of an investigation. The former findings support Fiske and Glick's (1995) argument that sexist attitudes predict judgments about unwanted social-sexual behaviors, as well as Franke's (1997) model of sexual harassment as a technology of sexism, which states that sexist beliefs are widespread in society, and sexual harassment punishes women and men who depart from traditional gender roles. According to Franke, what makes sexual harassment a form of sex discrimination is "not the fact that the conduct is sexual, but that sexual conduct is used to enforce or perpetrate gender norms and stereotypes" (p. 734). The latter findings by DeSouza, et al. (2007) are consistent with a previous study conducted by DeSouza and Solberg (2004) on man-to-man sexual harassment with U.S. college students. In both studies, college students who endorsed unwanted social-sexual behaviors between individuals of the same sex as sexual harassment were more likely than were those who did not endorse such behaviors as sexual harassment to agree that the target was sexually harassed and to agree that the case needed an investigation.

Initially the ruling made by the U.S. Supreme Court to expand the definition of sexual harassment to include same-sex sexual harassment in its 1998 decision *Oncale v. Sundowner Offshore Services* appeared to be a significant victory for LGBT individuals who desire, like every employee, to work in an environment free of harassment. Unfortunately, this has not come through, as LGBT employees still face hurdles to obtain remedy from the U.S. federal courts (Solberg & DeSouza, 2007). That is, since the 1998 *Oncale* decision, U.S. federal courts have ruled that if same-sex sexual harassment is based on the sexual orientation of the target rather than on the sexual desire of the perpetrator for the victim or on same sex animus by the perpetrator, then Title VII (1964) does not apply.

For example, in *Bibby v. Philadelphia Coca Cola Bottling Company* (2001), John Bibby sought remedy from the Court because he claimed that he was sexually harassed in a locker room by a co-worker who repeatedly yelled at him that "everybody knows you're gay as a three dollar bill," "everybody knows you're a faggot," and "everybody knows you take it up the ass." In addition, Bibby claimed that his supervisors harassed him by yelling at him, ignoring his reports of machinery problems, and enforcing rules against him in situations in which they were not enforced against Bibby's co-workers. Bibby also claimed that bathroom graffiti of a sexual nature relating to him was left on the walls much longer than other graffiti. He lost his case because the Court determined that he was not harassed because of his sex, but rather because of his sexual orientation, which the Court ruled was not a violation of Title VII. He appealed this ruling, but the Third Circuit Court upheld the decision. The Court noted that Congress has repeatedly rejected legislation that would extend Title VII to cover sexual orientation.

The current position of U.S. federal courts toward gay or lesbian targets of same-sex sexual harassment is contributing to the problem by allowing heterosexual perpetrators to escape with impunity. Such impunity reflects an institutional sanction of heterosexism and sexual prejudice. Solberg and DeSouza (2007) concluded that it is time for the U.S. Supreme Court or Congress to decide whether Title VII protects against sexual harassment based on the sexual orientation of the target.

The Contact Hypothesis

The contact hypothesis suggests that association with marginalized members of society (i.e., the "others" who belong to the "out-group" rather than to the "in-group" that constitutes mainstream society) may reduce prejudice against them (Allport, 1954). Thus, heterosexuals who interact with gay men and lesbians may develop positive attitudes toward homosexuality. In fact, several researchers have reported that heterosexuals who were prejudiced against gay men and lesbians had limited contact with them; conversely, having multiple and close personal contact with gay men and lesbians was related to positive attitudes toward them (e.g., Basow & Johnson, 2000; DeSouza, et al., 2007; Herek, 2000a, 2000b; Herek & Capitanio, 1996; Herek & Glunt, 1993). According to a public opinion poll in the United States, "[m]ore people know gays, see them on television, have them in their own family, and so they just begin to feel more comfortable with the idea" (Page, 2003, p. 10A).

Dixon, Durrheim, and Tredoux (2005) summarized the suggestions given in the contact literature in order to minimize prejudice toward out-group members (e.g., LGBT individuals):

- Contact should occur often.
- Contact should include similar numbers of in-group and out-group members.
- Contact should have real "acquaintance potential."
- Contact should happen across a wide range of social settings and situations.
- Contact should be free of competition.

- Contact should be evaluated as "valuable" to those involved.
- Contact should occur between individuals of the same or similar social standing.
- Contact should include counter-stereotypic out-group members.
- Contact should focus on cooperation in order to reach superordinate goals.
- Contact should be normatively and institutionally endorsed.
- Contact should be free from anxiety or other negative affect.
- Contact should be individualized and include the possibility of real friendship formation.
- Contact should include typical or average out-group members.

This is a long list of what should occur. In fact, Dixon, et al. (2005) criticized the contact hypothesis as being too idealistic, bearing little resemblance to the real world. They suggested that future research on the contact hypothesis should focus "on the mundane, seemingly unimportant, encounters that constitute the overwhelming majority of everyday contact experiences. This type of research would entail 'thick description' of unfolding interactions between groups in ordinary situations" (p. 703).

Conclusions

LGBT families challenge existing definitions of family. These "families dispute one of the central notions of family, namely the obligatory and strict linking of biological kinship with who constitutes being included in a definition of family" (Fitzgerald, 1999, p. 71). Moreover, the children of LGBT parents appear to benefit from the exposure to new and diverse points of view (e.g., gender roles and sexuality), as they seem to become interested in diversity, tolerance, and social justice not only with regard to sexual orientation, but also with regard to other social inequalities based on gender, race/ethnicity, and social class (Gartrell, et al., 2005; Miller, 1992).

LGBT parents also challenge existing psychological theories concerning family dynamics (e.g., psychoanalytic theories, social learning theories, and social cognitive theories), which highlight the importance of having both a mother and a father for normal child development (e.g., Fitzgerald, 1999). The earlier review of empirical studies with children of LGBT parents reported in this chapter does not support the view that heterosexual parents are essential for children's successful development, including the acquisition of gender-appropriate behavior (e.g., Golombok, et al., 2003). Overall, these children are resilient and thriving, as are their parents.

Future studies should further investigate, through multiple and rigorous research approaches, resiliency among LGBT individuals. For example, research on LGBT parents should not only investigate how they are comparable to heterosexual parents, but also focus on how LGBT parents are unique, and how such uniqueness may expand existing models of child-rearing practices, moral development, mental health, growth, spirituality, and fairness, to name a few. In addition, more studies comparing various within-groups that reflect the diversity of LGBT communities are necessary in order to find out similarities and differences on various outcome measures as a result of social class, race/ethnicity, culture, disability, and age factors. Cross-cultural studies will also increase our knowledge of same-sex couples and their children. For example, now it is possible to compare same-sex couples and their children in countries that have legalized same-sex marriage (e.g., Canada, Denmark, Great Britain, and the Netherlands) with same-sex couples and their children in countries where marriage equality is not yet a reality.

Last but not least, it is important to combat sexual prejudice in all spheres of life (e.g., employment, housing, military service, access to health care, and immigration, to name a few), including changing existing laws that perpetuate power differentials, which allow LGBT individuals to be treated as second-class citizens. Efforts to combat sexual prejudice by researchers and decision makers need to take a holistic or ecological approach by examining the impact of their research and decisions on individuals, families, institutions, communities, and society at large, as these systems are interrelated; that is, changes in one system will affect the dynamics in other systems. In addition, by addressing only one system, one may be implementing ineffective solutions. This review suggests that multiple forms of social inequalities need to be researched and confronted simultaneously.

If an LGBT individual or couple is considering becoming a parent or is facing a parenting contest, contact the National Lesbian and Gay Law Association at www.NLGLA.org to identify a lawyer licensed in your state who is familiar with LGBT family law.

References

Adams, W.L. (2006, May 23). Stats: Gay to wed. *Newsweek*. Retrieved on February 20, 2007, from http://www.msnbc.msn.com/id/7856685/site/newsweek/.

Allport, G.W. (1954). *The nature of prejudice*. Cambridge, MA: Addison-Wesley.

Associated Press. (2007a, February 5). *Ballot measure: Straight couples, procreate or else*. Retrieved on February 6, 2007, from http://www.onenewsnow.com/2007/02/homosexual_activists_would_req.ph.

Associated Press. (2007b, February 19). *Civil unions for gays now available in N.J.* Retrieved on February 21, 2007, from http://www.msnbc.msn.com/id/17224546.

Basow, S., & Johnson, K. (2000). Predictors of homophobia in female college students. *Sex Roles, 42*, 391–404.

Bibby v. Philadelphia Coca Cola Bottling Company, 260 F.3d 257 (Third Circuit 2001).

Brooks, D., & Goldberg, S. (2001). Gay and lesbian adoptive and foster care placements: Can they meet the needs of waiting children? *Social Work, 46*, 147–157.

Carter, K. (2006). The best interest test and child custody: Why transgender should not be a factor in custody determinations. *Health Matrix: Journal of Law Medicine, 16*, 209–236.

Dang, A., & Frazer, M.S. (2005). Black same-sex couple households in the 2000 U.S. Census: Implications in the debate over same-sex marriage. *Western Journal of Black Studies, 29,* 521–530.

DeSouza, E., & Solberg, J. (2004). Women's and men's reactions to man-to-man sexual harassment: Does the sexual orientation of the victim matter? *Sex Roles, 50,* 623–639.

DeSouza, E.R., Solberg, J., & Cerqueira, E. (2007). A cross-cultural perspective on judgments of woman-to-woman sexual harassment: Does sexual orientation matter? *Sex Roles 56,* 457–471.

Dixon, J., Durrheim, K., & Tredoux, C. (2005). Beyond the optimal contact strategy: A reality check for the contact hypothesis. *American Psychologist, 60,* 697–711.

Downs, A.C., & James, S.E. (2006). Gay, lesbian, and bisexual foster parents: Strengths and challenges for the child welfare system. *Child Welfare, 85,* 281–298.

Equal Employment Opportunity Commission. (2005, March 2). Sexual harassment. Retrieved January 16, 2007, from http://www.eeoc.gov/types/sexual_harassment.html.

Fiske, S.T., & Glick, P. (1995). Ambivalence and stereotypes cause sexual harassment: A theory with implications for organizational change. *Journal of Social Issues, 51,* 97–115.

Fitzgerald, B. (1999). Children of lesbian and gay parents: A review of the literature. *Marriage & Family Review, 29,* 57–75.

Franke, K.M. (1997). What's wrong with sexual harassment? *Stanford Law Review, 49,* 691–772.

Gallup Poll. (2005, April 19). Americans turn more negative toward same-sex marriage. Retrieved on February 13, 2007, from http://www.galluppoll.com/content/?ci=15889&pg=1.

Gartrell, N., Banks, A., Hamilton, J., Reed, N., Bishop, H., & Rodas, C. (1999). The National Lesbian Family Study: 2. Interviews with mothers of toddlers. *American Journal of Orthopsychiatry, 69,* 362–369.

Gartrell, N., Banks, A., Reed, N., Hamilton, J., Rodas, C., & Deck, A. (2000). The National Lesbian Family Study: 3. Interviews with mothers of five-year-olds. *American Journal of Orthopsychiatry, 70,* 542–548.

Gartrell, N., Deck, A., Rodas, C., Peyser, H., & Banks, A. (2005). The National Lesbian Family Study: 4. Interviews with the 10-year-old children. *American Journal of Orthopsychiatry, 75,* 518–524.

Gartrell, N., Hamilton, J., Banks, A., Mosbacher, D., Reed, N., Sparks, C., et al. (1996). The National Lesbian Family Study: 1. Interviews with prospective mothers. *American Journal of Orthopsychiatry, 66,* 272–281.

Glick, P., & Fiske, S.T. (1996). The Ambivalent Sexism Inventory: Differentiating hostile and benevolent sexism. *Journal of Personality and Social Psychology, 70,* 491–512.

Glick, P., & Fiske, S.T. (1997). Hostile and benevolent sexism: Measuring ambivalent sexist attitudes toward women. *Psychology of Women Quarterly, 21,* 119–135.

Golombok, S., Perry, B., Burston, A., Murray, C., Mooney-Somers, J., Stevens, M., et al. (2003). Children with lesbian parents: A community study. *Developmental Psychology, 39,* 20–33.

Gutek, B.A., & Done, R.S. (2001). Sexual harassment. In R.K. Unger (Ed.), *Handbook of the psychology of women and gender* (pp. 367–387). New York: Wiley.

Herek, G.M. (1994). Assessing heterosexuals' attitudes toward lesbians and gay men. In B. Greene & G.M. Herek (Eds.), *Lesbian and gay psychology: Theory, research, and clinical application* (pp. 206–228). Thousand Oaks, CA: Sage.

Herek, G.M. (2000a). The psychology of sexual prejudice. *Current Directions in Psychological Sciences, 9,* 19–22.

Herek, G.M. (2000b). Sexual prejudice and gender: Do heterosexuals' attitudes toward lesbians and gay men differ? *Journal of Social Issues, 56,* 251–266.

Herek, G.M. (2002). Gender gaps in public opinion about lesbians and gay men. *Public Opinion Quarterly, 66,* 40–66.

Herek, G.M. (2006). Legal recognition of same-sex relationships in the United States: A social science perspective. *American Psychologist, 61,* 607–621.

Herek, G.M., & Capitanio, J.P. (1996). "Some of my friends": Intergroup contact, concealable stigma, and heterosexuals' attitudes toward lesbians and gay men. *Personality and Social Psychology Bulletin, 22,* 412–424.

Herek, G.M., & Glunt, E.K. (1993). Interpersonal contact and heterosexuals' attitudes toward lesbians and gay men: Results from a national survey. *Journal of Sex Research, 30,* 239–244.

Kaiser Foundation (2001, November). Inside-OUT: A report on the experiences of lesbians, gays, and bisexuals in America and the public's views on issues and policies related to sexual orientation. Mento Park, CA.

Kerns, J.G., & Fine, M.A. (1994). The relation between gender and negative attitudes toward gay men and lesbians: Do gender role attitudes mediate this relation? *Sex Roles, 31,* 297–307.

Kilianski, S.E. (2003). Explaining heterosexual men's attitudes toward women and gay men: The theory of exclusively masculine identity. *Psychology of Men & Masculinity, 4,* 37–56.

Kitzinger, C., & Wilkinson, S. (2004). Social advocacy for equal marriage: The politics of "rights" and the psychology of "mental health." *Analyses of Social Issues and Public Policy, 4,* 173–194.

Kurdek, L.A. (2004). Are gay and lesbian cohabitating couples really different from heterosexual married couples? *Journal of Marriage & Family, 66,* 880–900.

Kurdek, L.A. (2005). What do we know about gay and lesbian couples? *Current Directions in Psychological Science, 14,* 251–254.

Maslow, A.H. (1968). *Toward a psychology of being* (2nd ed.). New York: Van Nostrand.

Masser, B., & Abrams, D. (1999). Contemporary sexism: The relationships among hostility, benevolence, and neosexism. *Psychology of Women Quarterly, 23,* 503–517.

Matthews, J.D., & Cramer, E.P. (2006). Envisaging the adoption process to strengthen gay- and lesbian-headed families: Recommendations for adoption professionals. *Child Welfare, 85,* 317–340.

McCreary, R. (1994). The male role and avoiding femininity. *Sex Roles, 31,* 517–531.

Miller, N. (1992). *Single parents by choice: A growing trend in family life.* New York: Insight Books.

Milville, M.L., & Fergunson, A.D. (2006). Intersections of sexism and heterosexism with racism. In M.G. Constantine & D.W. Sue (Eds.), *Addressing racism* (pp. 87–103). Hoboken, NJ: Wiley.

National Gay and Lesbian Task Force. (2006, November). *Anti-gay marriage measures in the U.S.* Retrieved on February 13, 2007, from http://www.thetaskforce.org.

National Gay and Lesbian Task Force. (2007, January). *State nondiscrimination laws in the U.S.* Retrieved on February 13, 2007, from http://www.thetaskforce.org.

Oncale v. Sundowner Offshore Services, Inc., 523 U.S. 75 (1998).

Page, S. (2003, July 28). Gay rights tough to sharpen into political "wedge issue": Shifting attitudes highlights risks for both parties. *USA Today*, p. 10A.

Patterson, C.J. (2000). Family relationships of lesbians and gay men. *Journal of Marriage and the Family, 62*, 1052–1069.

Patterson, C.J. (2004). Gay fathers. In M.E. Lamb (Ed.), *The role of the father in child development* (4th ed., pp. 397–416). New York: Wiley.

Peplau, L.A., & Beals, K.P. (2004). The family lives of lesbians and gay men. In A.L. Vangelisti (Ed.), *Handbook of family communication* (pp. 233–248). Mahwah, NJ: Erlbaum.

Pew Research Center for the People and the Press. (2005, August 3). Abortion and rights of terror suspects top court issues. Retrieved February 12, 2007, from http://people-press.org/reports/display.php3?ReportID=253.

Quinnipiac University Poll. (2006, November 22). *Same sex marriage.* Hamden, CT: Quinnipiac University Polling Institute. Retrieved February 14, 2007, from Polling the Nations database.

Richman, K. (2002). Lovers, legal strangers, and parents: Negotiating parental and sexual identity in family law. *Law and Society Review, 36*, 285–324.

Ryan, S.D., Pearlmutter, S., & Groza, V. (2004). Coming out of the closet: Opening agencies to gay and lesbian parents. *Social Work, 49*, 85–95.

Seltzer, R. (1992). The social location of those holding antihomosexual responses. *Sex Roles, 26*, 391–398.

Silverstein, L.B. (2002). Fathers and families. In J.P. McHale & W.S. Grolnick (Eds.), *Retrospect and prospect in the psychological study of families* (pp. 35–64). Mahwah, NJ: Lawrence.

Solberg, J.J., & DeSouza, E. (2007). An update on same-sex harassment since Oncale: Employees still face hurdles. *Journal of Law & Business, 13*, 55–69.

Title VII (1964). 42 U.S.C. Section 2000e et seq.

U.S. Census Bureau. (2000, April 1). Gateway to Census 2000. Washington, DC: Author. Retrieved February 19, 2007, from http://www.census.gov/main/www/cen2000.html.

U.S. General Accounting Office (2004, January 23). *Defense of Marriage Act: Update to prior report* (Document GAO-04-353R). Washington, DC: Author. Retrieved February 13, 2007, from http://www.gao.gov/new.items/d04353r.pdf.

Wainright, J.L., Russell, S.T., & Patterson, C.J. (2004). Psychosocial adjustment, school outcomes, and romantic relationships of adolescents with same-sex parents. *Child Development, 75*, 1886–1898.

Wester, S.R., Pionke, D.R., & Vogel, D.L. (2005). Male gender role conflict, gay men, and same-sex romantic relationships. *Psychology of Men & Masculinity, 6*, 195–208.

Whitley, B.E., Jr. (2001). Gender-role variables and attitudes toward homosexuality. *Sex Roles, 5*, 691–721.

CHAPTER 4

Culture and Work/Life Balance: Is There a Connection?

Presha E. Neidermeyer

We don't see things as they are, we see them as we are.

—Anais Nin

Nin's sentiment captures the essence of ethnocentrism: we view human behavior through the lens of our particular cultural experiences (King, 2002). Ethnocentrism involves placing more value on our own cultural norms than on those of other countries. Hofstede (1980) noted that individuals have a deceiving tendency to think, feel, and act from their own experiences. When they are placed in another cultural context, as for example when they work internationally, this tendency becomes especially apparent. One can, however, view other cultures from a cultural-relativistic perspective: noting that the values, beliefs, and life-styles of others represent their ways of adapting to the circumstances of their lives. A cultural-relativistic perspective is accepting of differences; it allows us to observe and to learn different attitudes, ways of behaving, and other aspects of life that characterize a group of individuals (Hofstede, 1980). Ideally, we gain insight into our *own* practices by being aware of, and sensitive to, the diverse approaches used by others.

One area of cultural distinctions where U.S. companies may be able to gain from foreign experiences is that of work/life balance. By employing a cultural-relativism stance, managers in the United States may be able to learn a great deal from the ways other countries treat issues such as child care responsibilities, parental leave, flextime, job sharing, time off from work, and the value of female as well as male employees. In this chapter, I use cultural variants on work/life issues in selected countries within the European Union (EU) to illustrate how the United States may be able to benefit from placing more value on families and those employees who take care of families.

The European Union and Work/Life Balance

The European Union presently comprises the following countries: Belgium, France, Luxembourg, Germany, Italy, the Netherlands, Denmark, Ireland, the United Kingdom, Greece, Portugal, Spain, Austria, Finland, Sweden, Cyprus, Czech Republic, Estonia, Hungary, Latvia, Lithuania, Malta, Poland, Slovakia, Slovenia, Bulgaria, and Romania. Several other countries have accession into the Union virtually guaranteed should they request it within the next decade.

A number of EU standards have a definite impact on work/life balance. Among these standards are the directive on parental leave, the directive on the protection of pregnant women (and those who are breastfeeding), the directive on child care, and the proposed directive on maximum working hours that would eliminate the "opt out" provisions of the European Union's current forty-eight-hour maximum workweek. And although work/life balance often is targeted somewhat narrowly on the relationship between work and parenting, the U.K. Department of Trade and Industry defines it more broadly as the coordination of the requirements of employment with those of life in general.

The six goals put forward by Macinnes (2005)—reduction in working time, ability to temporarily withdraw from work, providing child care, making sexual division of domestic and caring labor more equal, increasing the labor supply, and securing the labor supply over the long term (particularly in terms of the aging population by boosting fertility and sustaining family life)—underlie the debate that is currently under way within the European Union on revising the work time directive, which would provide basic protection for workers (European Parliament, 2006). The proposed directive is controversial, as the working day in Europe varies greatly from country to country.

Yet it is recognized at the policy level that adjusting the conditions under which people work across the different countries is central to achieving improved quality of work, greater productivity, and increased employment, which make up the Lisbon objectives (European Working Conditions Observatory, 2005).

I treat the six goals outlined by Macinnes individually below and follow that discussion with a look at benefits in selected EU countries.

Reduction in Working Time

Approximately 15 percent of Europeans are required to work more than forty-eight hours per week (Institute of Gerontology, 2003; this figure is represented by 20 percent male and 8 percent of female employees). At present in Europe, about 80 percent of the employees indicate that they are satisfied with their work/life balance. This percentage changes, however, for those employees working over 48 hours per week, where 44 percent report being unhappy with their work/life balance (European Working Conditions Observatory, 2005). Employees working regular and predictable hours rate their work/life balance most positively.

Studies suggest that the hours of work time may underestimate the hours that Europeans spend at work. Frequently, Latvians and Italians work a second job in order to boost income, and U.K. residents work unreported overtime (European Foundation for the Improvement of Living and Working Conditions, 2006b; Institute of Economic and Social Research, 2006a). The fact that most employees are satisfied with their present working conditions does not stop over half of them from wanting to reduce their working week by an average of 10 percent, while 10–15 percent desire to reduce the lifelong working hours (Institute of Gerontology, 2003).

A reduction in working hours may also mean that more flexible working hours would be desired. Indeed, 14 percent of full-time employees have made efforts to move into part-time work (European Working Conditions Observatory, 2005). The majority of employees, however, still work standard hours with 74 percent working the same number of hours per week and 61 percent having standard starting and finishing times (European Working Conditions Observatory, 2005). This indicates that employers have not yet picked up the desire or need for more flexibility in the workplace with regard to the hours spent at work.

It appears that European workers are most satisfied with their work/life balance when working standard hours encompassing no more than 48 hours per week. Employers in the United States could see a benefit in terms of work/life satisfaction by reducing overall working hours for their employees, since the workers in the United States work more overall hours than their European counterparts. Flexibility may well be the key to allowing employees to better balance their work/life responsibilities in both the United States and Europe as demands on employee time increase.

Ability to Temporarily Withdraw from Work

The ability to temporarily withdraw from work is vital for those employees who are balancing a family and work, particularly employees with infants. In response to this, the European Union has passed a policy on parental leave. The Directive of Parental Leave was adopted by the Council of the European Union in June 1996 and serves as binding legislation with which EU member states must comply. The Directive guarantees employees of all member states (except the United Kingdom), whatever their sex, the right to take parental leave to look after a child for at least three months following birth or adoption and ensures workers the right to return to the same or a similar job following parental leave. Member states may adopt legislation that is more favorable than the EU standard. The United Kingdom has now adopted new standards for maternity leave, effective April 2007, to allow for paid maternity leave up to thirty-nine weeks and the right to transfer a portion of this leave to the father provided the mother returns to work early (Cole & Carter, 2006).

The Council Directive on Protection of Pregnant Women, women who have recently given birth, and women who are breastfeeding was adopted in 1992; the Directive is binding on EU member states. It deals generally with the health and safety of women with respect to childbearing and breast-feeding. The directive includes provisions for modifying hours and ensuring appropriate leave, including a minimum of fourteen weeks of uninterrupted maternity leave, two weeks of which must be before delivery. It does not appear that the desire for a temporary termination of employment is solely accounted for by children, since over 20 percent of employees say that they would opt for a three-month sabbatical without pay (Institute of Gerontology, 2003).

U.S. employers should take note of the magnitude of paid leave following pregnancy in the European Union. While the law in the United States requiring that a job be held for a specified period of time is certainly better than nothing, in comparison to the benefits offered in the European Union this benefit is very minimal. It is particularly difficult for those with lower incomes or in single income households to do without a paycheck for any length of time.

Child Care

The Council Directive on Childcare was adopted in 1992 and is binding on EU member states. This directive is rather vague on the implementation of these topics, employers clearly have been put on notice that the governmental bodies are looking into the Lisbon objectives to protect the competitive environment in the European Union.

The engagement of the EU government in work/life policy should be noted by U.S. counterparts who are already behind in offering family-friendly benefits (such as paid maternity leave). They appear to be in peril of falling even further behind in the near future.

More Equal Distribution of Work between the Sexes

More men are found to be employed than women: 56 percent versus 44 percent. As evidenced in other studies (Institute of Gerontology, 2003; Institute of Economic and Social Research, 2006), when the traditional definition of work is expanded to include time spent in paying jobs, time spent commuting, and time spent doing unpaid work including child care, caring for elderly relatives and domestic duties, women work more hours than men even in the case of women engaged in part-time work.

The difference in working time between men and women varies across countries with reports indicating that women in Bulgaria and Romania spend eight more hours caring for children than males (ten as compared to two) and in the Scandinavian countries women spend nine more hours (sixteen as compared to seven). The additional hours spent by women in child care and other domestic duties is spent by men furthering their education (European Working Conditions Observatory, 2005).

Since women do the majority of the work outside the office in both the United States and the European Union, other policies need to be put in place, such as flexible working hours, in order to help individuals in balancing their work/life requirements if one wants to engage more women in the paid work force.

Increasing and Securing the Labor Supply

The demographics within Europe and the world are changing: the workplace is becoming older, more female, and more ethnically diverse (Hutton, 2005). Since females typically carry more of the domestic and child care duties, employers will have to adapt in order to retain and attract a qualified workforce. Longer working lives combined with longer life spans have made it more likely that employees are caring for elderly parents even while having young children at home (Hutton, 2005). Indeed, 40 percent of older employed women are considering retiring to take care of elderly family members (European Working Conditions Observatory, 2005).

Remuneration differences also exist between males and females in the European Union, with 50 percent of all female employees being positioned in the lower third of the income scale, while only 20 percent of their male counterparts occupy this same position. Men, on the other hand, are overrepresented in the upper third of the scale. This likely represents the higher prevalence of women in part-time work. However, while accounting for these differences, there still remain variations between full-time workers (European Working Conditions Observatory, 2005).

Employees in both the United States and the European Union need to be protected by law to ensure that there is equal pay for equal work between the sexes. Additionally, employers should institute policies in both the United States and the European Union to encourage flexibility in the workplace in scheduling and places of work to ensure that a competent workforce is retained while various circumstances are brought to bear on individual families. Equal pay and flexibility will both go a long way toward keeping people in the workforce.

These six issues will prove to be critical in developing a motivated and secure workforce into the future given that individuals now are beginning to demand more time outside work to spend as they see fit (Hutton, 2005). Cultural differences between countries may help to explain why employers are offering certain types of benefits to the employees.

Company Benefits

I have selected ten award-winning companies each in the United States, the United Kingdom, Germany, France, and Austria. From this list of fifty firms, forty-two had information on employee benefits on the company's home pages. I have used this information and summarized it in Table 4.1 to show what benefits are currently being rewarded in the workplace.

The benefits provided in the United States and the United Kingdom workplaces appear to be very similar. The three most frequently cited benefits were the same for the United States and the United Kingdom (medical, dental, and vision insurances; paid vacation and holidays; and retirement benefits). All benefits listed at a frequency equal to at least 50 percent in the United States were also mentioned in the United Kingdom with the exception of paid sick leave (not mentioned at all by United Kingdom employers), albeit to a lesser degree: disability insurance (40 percent United Kingdom), tuition reimbursement (20 percent United Kingdom), adoption assistance (20 percent United Kingdom), and employee assistance programs (20 percent United Kingdom). Disability insurance was listed by 60 percent of the

Table 4.1
Percentages of Award-Winning Workplaces Offering Specific Benefits*

	Total United States	Total United Kingdom	Total France	Total Germany	Total Austria
Medical and dental insurance	100%	80%	83%	30%	83%
Paid vacation or paid holidays	90%	80%	50%	70%	100%
Retirement, pension, 401(k) benefits	90%	90%	50%	20%	0%
Paid sick leave	80%	0%	50%	20%	33%
Life insurance	60%	80%	50%	20%	67%
Disability insurance	50%	40%	83%	70%	100%
Tuition reimbursement	50%	20%	33%	40%	17%
Adoption assistance	50%	20%	0%	0%	67%
Employee assistance programs	50%	20%	50%	70%	83%
Domestic partners benefit	20%	0%	17%	60%	83%
Award-winning workplace mentioned	20%	0%	17%	40%	67%
Nursing mother's room	10%	0%	33%	20%	67%
Employee associations	10%	0%	67%	0%	0%
Relocation allowance	0%	0%	50%	20%	0%
Additional services	0%	0%	17%	50%	33%

*Note: Award-winning firms from various countries selected ranged from a maximum of 10 firms to a minimum of 6 firms depending upon whether employee benefits were listed on the award-winning company's home page.

employers in the United States and 80 percent of employers in the United Kingdom.

The top three benefits in France were listed as medical, dental, and vision insurances (83 percent), disability insurance (83 percent), and employee associations (67 percent). A number of benefits were mentioned at least one-half the time within the employers' benefit charts and include paid vacation and holidays, retirement benefits, paid sick leave, life insurance, and relocation allowance (i.e., moving expenses). In Germany, the top three benefits all are mentioned by 70 percent of the employers and include retirement benefits, disability insurance, and employee assistance programs. Other benefits mentioned by over one-half the employers were domestic partners benefits and additional services provided to employees. In Austria, the top benefits were retirement programs and disability insurance (mentioned by 100 percent of the employers), medical, dental, and vision insurances, employee assistance programs, and domestic partners benefits (mentioned by 83 percent of employers). The other benefits included in company Web sites over one-half the time were life insurance, adoption assistance, award-winning workplaces, domestic partners benefits, and nursing mother's rooms (tied at 67 percent).

While there is a small level of differentiation in the workplace benefits offered among EU countries, there is a tremendous amount of overlap. This implies a growing consensus, at least in the perceptions of employers, as to the employee benefits that should be offered. Indeed, this is encouraging for employers attempting to attract individuals from beyond their borders in an attempt to get the most qualified applicants, since the benefits, rather than being country specific, appear to be markedly consistent.

It appears that companies within the European Union will be moving to offer a wider range of benefits to accommodate the desires of their employees and to attract/retain the necessary employee base within the coming years. If these companies continue to be vigilant in seeking out the types of benefits their employees desire and implement these policies quickly, the employee base within the European Union should continue to be well served and the European Union itself will be well under way to achieving the Lisbon objectives.

The United States, on the other hand, appears to be significantly behind in responding to the needs of its employees concerning work/life balance. This is particularly apparent in the comparison offered for maternity leave in the European Union as compared to the United States, as well as the average hours worked in the European Union versus the United States. Cultural relativism would suggest that in observing these alternate policies, U.S. employers might consider how different policies may influence the U.S. workforce positively, ultimately increasing satisfaction and productivity for employers.

References

Cole, K., & Carter, C. (2006). People management. p. 19. www.peoplemanagement
    .co.uk.
Crompton, R., & Lyonette, C. (2005). *Work-life "balance" in Europe*. ESRC GeNet
    Research Network.
Dowling, P., & Welch, D. (2004). *International human resource management: Managing
    people in a multinational context*. London: Thompson.
Employment Market Analysis and Research. (2006). *How have employees fared?
    Recent UK trends* (Research Series No. 56). London: UK Department of Trade
    and Industry.
European Foundation for the Improvement of Living and Working Conditions.
    (2006a). *Working time organisation under review*.
European Foundation for the Improvement of Living and Working Conditions.
    (2006b). *Working time and work-life balance in European companies*.
European Foundation for the Improvement of Living and Working Conditions.
    (2006c). *Long working hours and regular overtime*.
European Foundation for the Improvement of Living and Working Conditions.
    (2005a). *Quality in work and employment*.
European Foundation for the Improvement of Living and Working Conditions.
    (2005b). *Quality in work and employment*.
European Foundation for the Improvement of Living and Working Conditions.
    (2003). *Working-time preferences and work-life balance in the EU: Some policy consider-
    ations for enhancing the quality of life*.
European Parliament. (2006, October, 20). Working time and the work-life balance:
    How can we solve the dilemma? http://www.europarl.europa.eu.
European Working Conditions Observatory. (2005). *European working conditions sur-
    vey* (Fourth). Dublin: European Foundation for the Improvement of Living and
    Working Conditions.
Hofstede, G. (1980). Culture's consequences. Sage Publications Beverly Hills, CA.
Hutton, W. (2005, July, 5). A work-life balance for all? *CNN.com*, http://
    edition.cnn.com/2005/WORLD/europe/06/17/visionary.hutton/.
Institute of Economic and Social Research. (2006a). *Two in three workers work overtime
    to boost income*. European Foundation for the Improvement of Living and Working
    Conditions.
Institute of Economic and Social Research. (2006b). *Comparative survey on operating
    hours and working time*. European Foundation for the Improvement of Living and
    Working Conditions.
Institute of Gerontology, University of Dortmund, Germany. (2003). *A new organisa-
    tion of time over working life*. Dublin: European Foundation for the Improvement of
    Living and Working Conditions.
King, E. (2002). Ethnicity. In D. Levison, P. Cookson Jr., & Sadovnik, A. (Eds.), *Edu-
    cation and sociology: An encyclopedia*. (pp. 247–253). New York: Routledge Falmer.
Macinnes, J. (2005). Work-life balance in Europe: A response to the baby bust or
    reward for the baby boomers? *European Societies 8*, 223–249.
Mårtensson, M. (2007). European survey on working time and work-life balance:
    High levels of flexi-time arrangements in the UK compared to Europe. *The Occupa-
    tional Health & Safety Information Service*, Retrieved February 4, 2007, from http://
    uk.ihs.com/news/newsletters/ohsis.

TNS Infratest Sozialforschung, Germany. (2006). *Working time and work-life balance in European companies*. Dublin: European Foundation for the Improvement of Living and Working Conditions.

Trades Union Congress. (2005). *Research Trends: Work in the 21st Century?* http://www.tuc.org.uk/work_life/index.cfm?mins=475.

CHAPTER 5

Pregnancy Discrimination: Laboring under Assumptions in the Workplace*

Julie Manning Magid

Assumptions are made about pregnant women who work. For example, it is assumed that they will require extended leaves to give birth and care for their infants, change work patterns after giving birth, or have more than one child, thereby affecting their employer not once but possibly several times. Statistics can be found to support each of these assumptions. Working women in the United States who became first-time mothers from 1991 to 1994 averaged nearly three months leave after the birth of their child.[1] Mothers with infants under age one are more likely to work part-time than other women, and 45 percent do not participate in the workforce.[2] Many women bear more than one child; in the 1990s, U.S. fertility rates averaged two births per woman, an increase from the 1970s.[3]

These assumptions culminate in an idea that is devastating for pregnant working women—the assumption that their level of commitment to work is forever changed. This notion affects not just pregnant women but all women. An overwhelming majority of women will give birth at some point in their lives.[4] Thus from the moment women enter the workforce, they bear the weight of all these (statistically accurate) assumptions, which remain with them throughout most of their work lives.

Assumptions are often the source of pregnancy discrimination in the workforce. Statistics about women in the workplace help document trends and calculate averages but do not determine or predict how a given woman will organize her work life in relation to her family life. Each woman should make individual decisions about work and family based on her particular circumstances. If a woman is pregnant, the law should respect the dignity of her decisions concerning work and family by allowing her to work free from the burden of assumptions about parenting responsibilities and future pregnancies.

Employers run afoul of the law if the workplace environment is based on predetermined notions and expectations about how women should organize their work and families. Despite laws prohibiting pregnancy discrimination in the workplace, women believe preset notions about pregnancy and family life underlie employers' actions all too often. The number of pregnancy discrimination complaints filed with the Equal Employment Opportunity Commission (EEOC) increased nationwide by 10 percent between 2001 and 2002.[5] Although the number decreased slightly the following year, a long-term trend indicates complaints concerning discrimination based on pregnancy have risen 39 percent since 1992.[6] During the same time period, the nation's birth rate dropped by 9 percent. Pregnancy discrimination claims filed with the EEOC now climb each year at a rate exceeding the increase in filings for either sex discrimination or sexual harassment claims.

Why is pregnancy discrimination a growing concern? Employment trends suggest some reasons why the number of claims is increasing. More women now remain in their jobs while pregnant. In this era of leaner workforces, the time away from work often associated with pregnancy may create resentment. Managing parental leaves creates challenges for employers, particularly smaller ones. Finally, employers are less aware of prohibitions concerning pregnancy discrimination than of other federal discrimination laws.

Women represent about 47 percent of the labor force, and estimates are that the percentage will continue to grow.[7] While they are pregnant, women often remain in the workforce; in the 1990s, only 27 percent of pregnant women quit their jobs.[8] During the same decade, however, employers fired pregnant women at a higher rate than in the 1980s.[9] As more working women remain in their jobs while pregnant, incidents of discriminatory conduct rise. Women often resent the assumptions made about their work and family life and decide to file complaints when they determine the work environment is intolerable.[10]

Economic trends are related to the increase in pregnancy discrimination complaints. Productivity demands of lean workforces mean that employees work longer hours. If a woman takes maternity leave or other time off during pregnancy, overworked co-workers usually must share her job responsibilities. This is a particularly acute problem for smaller employers with fewer employees among whom additional work responsibilities can be divided.

In addition to the cost of lost productivity and efficiency during pregnancy or maternity leave, pregnancy raises employers' health insurance costs. However, pregnancy discrimination is expensive for employers too. In fiscal year 2005, the EEOC and state and local agencies collected $11.3 million from employers for violations of pregnancy discrimination laws.[11] This amount does not include the cost of litigation and damages paid when employees filed a lawsuit in federal or state courts.

The increase in complaints filed with the EEOC indicates that federal legislation has failed to end pregnancy discrimination. Although Congress attempted to include pregnancy discrimination as part of sex discrimination legislation generally, many courts interpret pregnancy discrimination law dissociated from gender stereotypes. Thus employers and employees alike are confused by varying interpretations of the legal parameters. More recent legislation used a gender-neutral approach to prohibiting discrimination based on family-related commitments. However, this approach did not account for the biological reality of childbirth and resulted in the unintended consequence of making it more difficult for women to maintain legislative protection than men.

An overview of pregnancy discrimination law's laborious development is described in this chapter. Uncertainties remain concerning the legality of crucial employer policies and procedures. Organizations' efforts to comply with antidiscrimination legislation are compromised by the lack of clarity of the underlying statutes and the differing interpretations. This chapter highlights the areas of greatest ambiguity concerning pregnancy discrimination law. In addition, the overlap between federal family leave legislation is analyzed. Two of the most important issues emerging in the context of pregnant employees—benefits policies and defining which aspects of motherhood are included in pregnancy discrimination legislation—are assessed.

Before turning to the legislative landscape, however, a recent court decision provides an example of the assumptions that prevent women from contributing to an organization. Eliminating these assumptions, as demanded by the court in this case, offers the best opportunity to promote organizational excellence and workplace equity.

Compared to other types of discrimination, that based on pregnancy is less well known. Although the Civil Rights Act of 1964 prohibited sex discrimination in employment, the U.S. Supreme Court did not interpret sex discrimination as including differential treatment based on pregnancy. In 1978, fourteen years after Congress passed this major federal antidiscrimination law, it was amended to include pregnancy.

Unfortunately, courts interpreting pregnancy discrimination law have reached vastly different conclusions concerning the parameters of this protection.[12] Some interpret pregnancy discrimination bans narrowly so that many pregnant women have no opportunity to redress this type of workplace discrimination. Although other courts take a broader view concerning the types of employment actions that are prohibited legally, these different interpretations leave employers and employees alike confused about the law and the nature of pregnancy discrimination. The increasing number of pregnancy discrimination complaints filed with the EEOC and federal courts indicates a wide range of conduct result in women seeking to redress discrimination through the law.

Elana Back, an elementary school psychologist who filed a discrimination claim against her employer for assumptions about her commitment to work following her pregnancy, had received several positive performance reviews. Following the birth of her first child and three months of maternity leave, however, Back's career path derailed due to her employer's concern that she could not be a good mother and remain devoted to her job. Back believed that her supervisor relied on predetermined notions about women and their family responsibilities to inquire repeatedly about her plans for additional pregnancies. In particular, the supervisor asked about how Back would "space" her pregnancies, requested that she not become pregnant again until the supervisor retired, and suggested that Back should wait until her first child was in kindergarten before conceiving again.

As Back approached job tenure, her supervisor expressed growing concern about her work and family priorities. The supervisor told Back that it was impossible to be a good mother and have her job. In addition, the supervisor was concerned that after the school awarded Back tenure, her level of job commitment would drop because she had "little ones at home." The supervisor believed another year before recommending tenure would give her time to assess Back's child care situation.[13]

Back asked a federal court, the Court of Appeals for the Second Circuit, to determine whether her employer's stereotypical statements and actions about motherhood and the qualities of a good mother were a form of gender discrimination. The Second Circuit concluded that questioning a woman's abilities and workplace commitment based on her status as a mother strikes at the heart of gender stereotyping. The court referenced a recent U.S. Supreme Court decision that characterized persistent generalizations based on gender, such as those Back described, as the fault line between work and family life that is an enduring obstacle in employment opportunity.[14] The court held that "the notions that mothers are insufficiently devoted to work, and that work and motherhood are incompatible, are properly considered to be, themselves, gender-based."[15]

Although the ruling in the *Back* decision is limited to the states within the Second Circuit, nonetheless, the court's recognition of the link between gender and pregnancy—including postpregnancy assumptions about family planning and responsibilities—is an important step toward reuniting pregnancy discrimination law with gender discrimination. All too often, assumptions about women in the workplace correspond with those about their role as mothers. The history of gender discrimination law, however, shows a concerted effort to dissociate gender discrimination from pregnancy and parenting. Such dissociation ignores the reality of women's experience in the workplace.

When Congress enacted Title VII of the Civil Rights Act of 1964 to address employment discrimination based on race, color, religion, sex, and

national origin,[16] pregnancy discrimination received no specific consideration. In fact, the legislative history of Title VII suggests that some members
of Congress did not intend to include sex as a protected class. Congressman
Howard Smith of Virginia, a representative with little commitment to the
civil rights bill, amended the pending legislation to include sex as a protected
class in what some speculate was a maneuver to defeat the law's passage.[17]
Following Smith's amendment, debate concerning the amendment was light-
hearted and humorous.[18] Although Title VII survived with the amendment
intact, the less-than-serious discussion concerning protection from gender
discrimination left only a brief and often unhelpful legislative history.[19]

The EEOC, the agency responsible for administering Title VII, issued
inconsistent interpretations concerning the role pregnancy played in gender
discrimination. Initial EEOC opinions permitted maternity, pregnancy, and
childbirth exclusions from employers' benefit plans under Title VII. By
1972, however, the EEOC reversed its earlier opinions and promulgated
guidelines indicating that pregnancy, childbirth and recovery, and related
medical conditions had to be treated the same as other temporary disabilities
for insurance purposes in employee benefit plans. Thus, if an employer's
plan provided time off for other temporary disabilities, it also had to allow
women the same amount of time for temporary disability for pregnancy-
related reasons.

The Supreme Court addressed pregnancy discrimination within the meaning of Title VII in a 1976 case, *General Electric v. Gilbert* (referred to as *Gilbert*). In that case, a group of female employees filed a lawsuit against their
employer based on its insurance plan. It covered employees who became disabled due to illness or injury. It also covered procedures specific to male
reproduction, such as vasectomies, but excluded disabilities resulting from
pregnancy. The female employees claimed this exclusion violated Title VII.

In the *Gilbert* decision, the Supreme Court determined that discrimination
because of sex, as prohibited by Title VII legislation, did not include pregnancy discrimination. The Court reasoned that the employer's insurance policy excluding pregnancy disability did not distinguish between males and
females but between "pregnant persons and non-pregnant persons." This
was not understood to represent a gender-based classification because the
group of nonpregnant persons included both men and women. The Court
found pregnancy was not "a disease or disability comparable in all other
respects to covered diseases or disabilities and yet confined to the members
of one sex or race."[20] This ruling denied disability coverage to pregnant
women under the private employer's insurance plans. In an earlier case, the
Court upheld an exclusion of pregnant women from disability coverage under
a state insurance plan.[21]

Not all members of the Court agreed with the *Gilbert* decision. Justice William Brennan authored a dissenting opinion that asserted the Court had lost
sight of Title VII's intent when it held that pregnancy discrimination was
not gender discrimination. Brennan appealed for the Court to approach the

issue with a broader understanding of gender. In the dissenting opinion he wrote, "surely it offends common sense to suggest that a classification revolving around pregnancy is not, at a minimum, strongly 'sex related.'"[22] Similarly, Justice John Paul Stevens's dissenting opinion rejected dividing the pool of employees into pregnant women and nonpregnant persons. Instead, he argued for an implicit recognition that biological females cannot be dissociated from the reality of pregnancy. Stevens stated: "The classification is between persons who face a risk of pregnancy and those who do not."[23]

The dissents by Brennan and Stevens received full vindication when Congress responded to the *Gilbert* decision by amending Title VII "to prohibit sex discrimination on the basis of pregnancy." The House and Senate Reports specifically acknowledged that Brennan's and Stevens's dissents reflected congressional intent in enacting Title VII. The Pregnancy Discrimination Act (PDA) amended Title VII by providing that

> the terms "because of sex" or "on the basis of sex" include, but are not limited to, because of or on the basis of pregnancy, childbirth, or related medical conditions; *and* women affected by pregnancy, childbirth, or related medical conditions shall be treated the same for all employment-related purposes, including receipt of benefits under fringe benefit programs, as other persons not so affected but similar in their ability or inability to work.[24]

The PDA's dual purpose of addressing the definition of sex discrimination and overruling the controversial *Gilbert* decision is evident in the congressional committee reports as well as the language of the amendment. The bill "was introduced to change the definition of sex discrimination in Title VII to the commonsense view and to ensure that working women are protected."[25] The Supreme Court recognized Congress's expression of its intent to prohibit discrimination based on pregnancy by enacting the PDA.[26] The Court noted the act's proponents "repeatedly emphasized that the Supreme Court had erroneously interpreted congressional intent and that amending legislation was necessary to reestablish the principles of Title VII law as they had been understood prior to the *Gilbert* decision."[27]

In a later case, the Court debated whether the PDA preempted a California statute requiring employers to provide four months of unpaid maternity leave and guaranteed reinstatement to pregnant employees.[28] If the PDA had preempted the statute, states could not mandate broader pregnancy discrimination laws than the PDA. With a fractured majority, the Court concluded Congress did not mean to prohibit employers from giving preferential treatment to pregnant employees in enacting the PDA. Instead, the Court emphasized the broad goals of the PDA by noting, "rather than limiting existing Title VII principles and objectives, the PDA extends them to cover pregnancy."[29] As a result of this decision, some states require private employers to provide rights to its pregnant employees beyond those identified in the PDA.

Defining the prohibitions under the PDA has proved challenging. For instance, does it apply to women who are not pregnant? Mary Craig was one such woman. She had a decision to make in 1982. She could lose her job or be sterilized and present evidence of her sterility to her employer. Her co-worker, Elsie Nason, was not willing to be sterilized to keep her job and because of that, she received less pay in a job to which she was involuntarily transferred. Another co-worker, Donald Penney, however, did not receive a requested leave from his job. He was required to remain in a position that threatened his future children through high lead exposure. These are the representatives of the class who challenged their employer's fetal protection policy by filing a federal lawsuit.[30]

The employer, a battery manufacturer, had a valid concern about its legal liability. During the manufacturing process, employees were exposed to lead.

The Occupational Safety and Health Administration had determined that such exposure sometimes resulted in blood lead levels exceeding the critical level for an employee who planned to have biological children. Parents' high levels of exposure to lead increased the risk that their children would suffer serious birth defects. After eight of its employees became pregnant with blood lead levels regularly exceeding the critical level, the employer instituted a new policy affecting all women employees (although male exposure could result in birth defects of biological children as well): "It is policy that women who are pregnant or who are capable of bearing children will not be placed into jobs involving lead exposure or which could expose them to lead through the exercise of job bidding, bumping, transfer or promotion rights."[31]

One federal appeals court judge characterized this case as "likely the most important sex-discrimination case in any court since 1964, when Congress enacted Title VII."[32] None of the three employees who filed the lawsuit was pregnant or planned on becoming pregnant. Mary Craig chose sterilization to comply with the company policy and therefore was medically incapable of becoming pregnant. Nonetheless, their status as nonpregnant persons did not exclude them from the discrimination prohibitions under Title VII as amended by the PDA. The Supreme Court noted the employer's policy explicitly categorized employees based on the "potential for pregnancy," "[The company] has chosen to treat all of its female employees as potentially pregnant; that choice evinces discrimination on the basis of sex."[33] The Court found this stereotype of women goes to the very heart of what is prohibited by the PDA: "Congress in the PDA prohibited discrimination on the basis of a woman's ability to become pregnant. We do no more than hold that the PDA means what it says."[34]

The law is clear, then, that employers cannot institute employment policies that single out female employees based on the assumption that these employees may become pregnant. They cannot bar women, but not men, from jobs involving exposure to substances known to harm the human reproductive system. Less clear and far more problematic are the decisions made about employees who are pregnant and require leave. The wording of the PDA is convoluted and subject to differing interpretations. Specifically, courts have long discussed whether Congress intended the amendment broadly to incorporate pregnancy with gender discrimination or if the PDA addresses more specifically the medical leave associated with pregnancy and childbirth.

The debate arises from the specific language of the PDA, which was quoted earlier. Two clauses are joined by the conjunction *and*. Often these clauses are read together to limit the PDA to outlawing discrimination only as it relates to the disability associated with pregnancy. In this interpretation, the conjunction is defined as meaning "therefore." That interpretation unnecessarily narrows the discrimination that women encounter in the workplace. The reading of the clauses of the PDA most supported by the legislative history and the Supreme Court's rulings is to consider them independently. The meaning of the first clause is not limited by the specific language in the second. This interpretation means the conjunction is defined as "in addition," a more common definition of *and* than "therefore." The second clause directly overturns the *Gilbert* case by explaining the application of the general principle to women employees disabled by pregnancy, childbirth, and related conditions.[35]

Perhaps the most notable decision limiting the language of the PDA to disability leave concerns a department store employee. The following federal Court of Appeals decision is notable due to its narrow interpretation of pregnancy discrimination and its impact on decisions concerning pregnancy discrimination claims filed in many federal courts. A department store fired its pregnant employee, Kimberly Hern Troupe, one day before her scheduled maternity leave. Her employer stated the termination was not due to pregnancy but due to repeated absences and tardiness caused by her severe morning sickness. The employee countered that the employer's explanation for termination was nonsensical given that she was one day away from the maternity leave that would resolve the issue of morning sickness. The court drew a now often cited comparison to resolve this issue:

> Suppose that Lord & Taylor had an employee named Jones, a black employee scheduled to take a three-month paid sick leave for a kidney transplant; and whether thinking that he would not return to work when his leave was up or not wanting to incur the expense of paying him while he was on sick leave, the company fired him. In doing so...the company could not be found guilty of racial discrimination unless...there was evidence that it failed to exhibit comparable rapacity toward similarly situated employees of the white race.[36]

This example of a black employee in need of a kidney transplant is irrelevant to the situation of an employee who no longer will need leave following giving birth. As a commentator has described the difference, "the black kidney patient does not undergo transplant surgery because he is black. Rather, he happens to be a man of color who also needs a kidney transplant. A working woman like Troupe, on the other hand, must take a maternity leave precisely for the reason that the law protects her from discrimination: her pregnancy."[37] Nonetheless, other courts adopted this rationale in pregnancy discrimination cases. In doing so, several courts support the rationale first voiced by the court deciding Troupe's claim of pregnancy discrimination: "Employers can treat pregnant women as badly as they treat similarly affected but non-pregnant employees."[38]

However, pregnancy is not the same as other employees' disabilities. As one judge noted, "if Congress intended to equate pregnancy with a temporary disability...it afforded pregnant women precious little protection when it enacted the PDA."[39] Characterizing pregnancy as a disability further dissociates pregnancy from the reality of women in the workplace. Assumptions concerning loyalty to the job, future time off, and parenting are not made when an employee needs a kidney transplant. Pregnancy is unique in these assumptions and in the gender it affects. Furthermore, most individuals do not intend to become disabled or expect it as a logical result of their actions. Pregnancy often is an intended and expected result.

Therefore, although no one would suggest Jones should consider the impact medical leave will have on his job in deciding whether to have a kidney transplant, employers often expect women to consider timing of pregnancies to minimize the impact on their job. As one court noted about a comparison between men on sick leave and women on maternity leave, "the men were incapacitated while the women were not....One can draw no valid comparison between people, male or female, suffering extended incapacity from illness or injury and young mothers wishing to nurse little babies."[40] As this opinion indicates, disability is considered a more acceptable reason to take time away from work than leave associated with pregnancy. Unfortunately, women's pregnancy-related leaves too often are viewed as an admission of women's disinterest in their work or career.

A comparison between pregnancy and disability is inappropriate because the former is plagued by unique stereotypes and assumptions that include not only pregnancy itself but also motherhood and childrearing. By its nature, however, pregnancy carried to term will result in a short-term medical disability. Nonetheless, some courts hold this disability is not covered by the PDA and that the PDA does not include protection of pregnant employees' jobs if the employees take time away from work. The recovery from pregnancy, although medically recognized, is not consistently interpreted as protected by the PDA's discrimination prohibitions. One court rejected the claim that more than one week of incapacitation was required after giving birth.[41] However, other courts hold this narrow interpretation of the PDA is a violation of the letter as well as the spirit of Title VII and the PDA.[42] "A short-term inability to work is bound up with the very nature of pregnancy and childbirth" and it is therefore a violation of the PDA to dismiss an employee for taking leave under the PDA.[43]

The PDA, according to a federal Court of Appeals, "was not designed to handcuff employers by forcing them to wait until an employee's pregnancy causes a special economic disadvantage."[44] Instead, the court noted that the bank employing Jessica Maldonando as a part-time teller would not violate the PDA by terminating her if her pregnancy leave would affect the bank's functioning. The court held that "an employer cannot take anticipatory adverse action[45] against a pregnant employee," however, "an employer may ...project the normal inconveniences of pregnancy and their secondary effects in the future and take actions in accordance with and in proportion to those predictions."[46] The "normal inconveniences" that may result in adverse action, including termination of a pregnant employee, include "the need to take more frequent snack and restroom breaks and the need to take some time off, at the very least, to give birth."[47]

This conclusion is perhaps understandable given the fundamental misunderstanding of the PDA's purpose. The court deciding Maldonado's discrimination claim posited that "the PDA was designed to allow individual women to make independent choices about whether to continue to work while pregnant."[48] This statement is not a true reflection of the congressional record when Congress amended Title VII to explicitly include pregnancy as gender discrimination. Rather, a sponsor of the PDA, Senator Williams, explained that the "entire thrust" of the PDA "is to guarantee women the basic right to participate fully and equally in the workforce, without denying them the fundamental right to full participation in family life."[49] Representative Tsongas stated, "Title VII and the PDA are designed to 'put an end to an unrealistic and unfair system that forces women to choose between family and career.'"[50] An employer who terminates an employee because she needs time off to give birth is forcing the employee and her family to choose between work and family.

A division exists between those federal appellate courts that hold pregnancy requires employers to grant some leave for the disability associated with giving birth and those that hold the PDA does not require any leave for pregnant employees if the employer does not offer leave to other employees with similar temporary disabilities. Therefore, a pregnant employee's job may depend on where she lives, not federal law.

In 1993, Congress implicitly acknowledged that Title VII—and the PDA specifically—failed to eliminate pregnancy discrimination. Therefore, it enacted new federal legislation to address the issue of pregnancy as well as other disabilities and family care–related leaves. As a whole, the legislation promoted work and family life balance but failed to address some of the most pressing pregnancy discrimination concerns.

The Family and Medical Leave Act of 1993 (FMLA) offered far more comprehensive protection concerning employment policies affecting pregnancy and maternity leave than the PDA.[51] By specifying leave provisions related to pregnancy and childbirth, it clarified for affected employers their obligations concerning pregnant employees. After holding hearings concerning parental leave, Congress determined that "historically, denial or curtailment of women's employment opportunities has been traceable directly to the pervasive presumption that women are mothers first and workers second. This prevailing ideology about women's roles has in turn justified discrimination against women when they are mothers or mothers-to-be."[52] The FMLA was enacted to minimize the potential for discrimination against women by making leave for family related commitments available to everyone, regardless of gender.

The FMLA requires employers to allow employees to return to work following a leave for the birth of a child, adoption of a child, or the serious health condition of employees or members of the employees' immediate family. It eliminates the difficulty in taking leave for prenatal care or childbirth and the confusion about whether such leave is required by the PDA by specifically addressing these aspects of pregnancy. Typically, employers may require employees to have their health care providers certify that their requests for leave meet the parameters of the FMLA. Employees must notify employers of the need for leave in advance. However, Congress recognized the unique needs of pregnant employees by providing some latitude from these documentation requirements.[53]

Under the FMLA, pregnant employees can miss work for morning sickness without obtaining a doctor's note. Absences related to pregnancy and prenatal care are permitted in short time increments. Therefore, an employee who is protected by the FMLA may arrive to work one hour late every day if she is ill as a result of her pregnancy, and her employer may not take any disciplinary action against her. Similarly, that employee may be late to work one day, leave at noon the following day, and continue that pattern for weeks, all without discipline or other adverse employment action.

Although the FMLA is important legislation, it has several important drawbacks. First, it only applies to employers who have fifty or more full-time employees for twenty or more calendar weeks. This includes the largest employers but excludes most employees. Second, and importantly for working women, the FMLA only covers employees who have been employed full-time for at least one year. The firing of Troupe one day before her maternity leave and Maldonado if she would have asked for a day off to give birth would not have violated the FMLA. Neither Troupe nor Maldonado was employed full-time for one year when terminated.

One way Congress tried to consider employers' needs was by requiring employees to work full-time for one year before receiving the benefits of the FMLA. Congress also attempted to end the stigma associated with family leave by making it available to both sexes. However, the FMLA has the unintended consequence of perpetuating women's career stagnation based on pregnancy. It prevents many women from changing jobs to advance their careers and increase their earning power because of its limited coverage. Although men who take family leave when a child is born most likely do not need it before that time, women may need leave throughout the pregnancy. Therefore, to be protected by the FMLA they must work twelve months before conceiving. The inexact nature of conception makes many women leery of changing jobs if they believe they might conceive prior to their first twelve months of employment. Retaining parental leave protection is more difficult for women than for men, but the FMLA coverage provisions do not recognize this gap in coverage. A gender-neutral approach to family leave protection ignores the reality that working women may become pregnant throughout the majority of their working lives.

In addition to limitations concerning the employees covered by the FMLA, the leave it guarantees is limited to twelve weeks in a twelve-month period and is unpaid. Each increment of absence, whether fifteen minutes or several hours, is counted toward the total of twelve weeks. This is both an administrative problem for many employers and a disadvantage of the FMLA for employees who have difficult pregnancies. Absences during pregnancy count against the time employees have to recover from childbirth and care for their infants. Women suffering complications of pregnancy may deplete their entire leaves before their infants are born. Because FMLA leaves are unpaid, financial concerns may prevent women from taking additional leave even if their employers permit an extension. Women's short-term medical disability following childbirth does not entitle them to additional leave time. After the twelve-week total, they must return to work or risk termination.

The Supreme Court described the FMLA as a positive advance to eliminate the stereotypes confronting working women.

> By creating an across-the-board, routine employment benefit for all employees, Congress sought to ensure that family-care leave would no longer be stigmatized as an inordinate drain on the workplace caused by female employees, and that employers could not evade leave obligations simply by hiring men. By setting a minimum standard of family leave for all eligible employees, irrespective of gender, the FMLA attacks the formerly state-sanctioned stereotype that only women are responsible for family care-giving, thereby reducing employers' incentive to engage in discrimination by basing hiring and promotion decisions on stereotypes.[54]

The Court extended FMLA coverage to state employees and large private employers after agreeing that Congress, in legislative hearings prior to passage of the FMLA, recorded a pattern of state constitutional violations based on gender discrimination. The Court found the FMLA was an appropriate remedy for these violations because statutes such as Title VII that merely demanded gender equality without requiring any actions to achieve that result had proved ineffective.[55]

Despite congressional efforts to make pregnancy a more gender-neutral event by passing the FMLA, the biological reality is that pregnancy affects women, and gender distinctions remain barriers to their employment opportunities. An issue receiving much attention in this regard is the exclusion of contraception from employers' benefit plans. Courts have revisited the PDA and Title VII to test the intersection of employer's insurance plans and sex discrimination based on pregnancy-related issues. In *Erickson v. Bartell Drug Co.*, the employer no longer requires employees to avoid childbearing to qualify for the best jobs, as did the employer in *Gilbert*, but an employee is seeking employer support of her decision not to have children.[56] The resulting issue is whether the PDA and Title VII address pregnancy prevention rather than pregnancy or the capacity to become pregnant.

Bartell Drug, an employer in Washington state, included a comprehensive prescription plan in its employee benefits package. The plan was self-insured and covered all prescription drugs, including several preventive drugs and devices, such as blood pressure-and cholesterol-lowering drugs, hormone replacement therapies, prenatal vitamins, and drugs to prevent allergic reactions, breast cancer, and blood clotting. It specifically excluded a handful of products, including contraceptive devices such as birth control pills, Norplant, Depo-Provera, intrauterine devices, and diaphragms. Prescribed weight reduction, infertility, smoking cessation, and experimental drugs also were excluded, as were dermatological treatments for cosmetic purposes and growth hormones.

The employer maintained that its prescription plan was unrelated to the gender equality provisions of Title VII and the PDA. The district court disagreed, stating:

> The legislative history of Title VII does not forecast how the law was to be interpreted by future courts faced with specific examples of allegedly discriminatory conduct. The truth of the matter is, Congress' intent regarding the evolution of a law is rarely apparent from fragments of legislative history. Long before this particular dispute arose, the protections of Title VII had no doubt been applied in ways that were never anticipated by the Representatives and Senators who voted for it or the President who signed it into law. Nevertheless, Congress has generally chosen to interfere with the judiciary's interpretation of Title VII only where the courts attempted to restrict its application.[57]

Although the control of fertility, enabled by the excluded contraceptives, does not correlate with the terms of "pregnancy, childbirth or related medical conditions" in the language of the PDA, the district court interpreted this provision broadly based on the PDA's history. It found that Congress "clearly had in mind the obvious and then-commonplace practice of discriminating against women in all aspects of employment, from hiring to the provisions of fringe benefits, based on an assumption that women would get pregnant and leave the workforce."[58] Sex-based categorization violates Title VII as amended by the PDA. The court ruled that exclusion of a woman-only benefit, such as female contraception, from a comprehensive prescription benefit plan is sex discrimination in violation of federal law.

This case represented the first time a federal court ruled on the issue of contraception exclusion from a prescription plan. As a district court decision, the ruling is limited to western Washington state. However, the EEOC reached the same decision in a similar case. Although EEOC decisions are not binding on courts interpreting the law, they carry some weight with the courts, as the following EEOC decision did with the *Erickson* court.

The EEOC heard a case brought by nurses whose employer did not cover contraception in its health insurance plan. In finding this exclusion discriminatory, the EEOC reasoned that only women can become pregnant. This gender distinction cannot, under employment discrimination laws, affect women's terms and conditions of employment in any way. "Contraception is a means by which a woman controls her ability to become pregnant. The PDA's prohibition on discrimination against women based on their ability to become pregnant thus necessarily includes a prohibition on discrimination related to a woman's use of contraceptives."[59]

The EEOC found additional support for this contention from language in the PDA exempting employers from any obligation to pay for abortions. If Congress explicitly made this exception, Congress also could have exempted employers from an obligation to include contraception in their benefit plans but did not. Therefore, employers providing benefits must do so without discriminating under the PDA.

Increasingly, state law prohibits many employers from excluding prescription contraceptives from comprehensive insurance coverage of prescriptions. The state laws generally require insurance plans to provide equal coverage for FDA-approved prescription contraceptives and related outpatient care as other preventive prescription drugs and outpatient care.[60] Many employees do not benefit from these state laws, however, because federal law governs employers who are self-insured.[61] Therefore, future court decisions will determine how broadly the PDA is interpreted in instances of contraceptive exclusion from an employer's benefit plan.

Another emerging issue concerning pregnancy discrimination focuses on defining when it starts and ends. One view is that pregnancy is an easily definable biological condition. While the biological condition exists, adverse employment action based on the pregnancy itself is prohibited. Related implications of pregnancy, such as absence not covered by the FMLA, are not based on the pregnancy but on the employer's expectations of job performance. As one court has described it, firing a pregnant employee because of excessive absences due to pregnancy-related illness is harsh but is not discrimination.[62] This rationale is based on the assumption the employer would terminate any employee with excessive absences. This of course ignores the stereotypes and preset notions that Congress recognized were associated with pregnancy when it enacted both the PDA and the FMLA.

If pregnancy is not purely a biological condition but a gender distinction that includes conception, as some courts recognize, what other elements of a working woman's life are associated with pregnancy? Assumptions about working mothers with infants increasingly are the source of complaints filed with the EEOC and the courts.

The typical scenario is that experienced by Celena Venturelli when she was pregnant and working as a temporary employee in a not-for-profit corporation. Her supervisors were impressed by her work and decided to offer her a permanent position. When a supervisor met with her to discuss the permanent job offer, the discussion was not about employment but about her impending status as a new mother. The supervisor maintained he wanted to be sensitive to Venturelli's pregnancy and not make her feel that the employer was rushing her into larger responsibilities. If this was the intent, it was not what was communicated in the conversation. Instead, the supervisor discussed in detail Venturelli's pregnancy and how she would deal with it in a permanent job with the employer. He made comments about women changing their minds about working after they hold their babies in their arms. The supervisor suggested she take the time necessary to stay at home with her child.

Venturelli was stunned into silence. Rather than viewing the discussion as sensitivity to her situation, she was offended by the stereotypes of mothers that were irrelevant to offering her a permanent job. After this conversation, Venturelli no longer wanted the job she once hoped for because she did not want to work for a discriminatory employer. The employer lost the individual it determined was the best candidate for the job because of the supervisor's conduct.[63]

Many courts view pervasive assumptions about a new mother's work life as "callous" but not discriminatory.[64] Supervisors' expressions that a woman will not return to work full-time after having a baby are insufficient evidence of pregnancy discrimination.[65] Instead, some discriminatory action during pregnancy often is required. For instance, a district manager's instructions to others to reduce efforts to train a pregnant employee due to the manager's doubts about whether she would return from maternity leave could constitute evidence of discrimination. The employee did not receive training because of her pregnancy.[66]

Requiring such a close connection to action during pregnancy directly contradicts the congressional record concerning passage of the PDA. Congress intended the PDA to address "the assumption that women will become [pregnant] and leave the labor force [which] leads to the view of women as marginal workers, and is at the root of the discriminatory practices which keep women in low-paying and dead-end jobs."[67] These interpretations of pregnancy discrimination allow assumptions to eliminate women's decisions about organizing work and family. Such assumptions negatively impact the family generally, making this an issue affecting both men and women.

For women to participate fully in the workforce, pregnancy discrimination must confront the assumptions and stereotypes surrounding roles of mother or caregiver. Even the most conscientious and concerned employer, as Venturelli's supervisor professed to be, may create a difficult work environment because pervasive stereotypes are accepted as the norm in the workplace. Employers must understand these stereotypes and accept each woman's individual decision about whether to have children and how to be a parent.

The major challenge for working women today is to make decisions about their family relationships free from the weight of expectations and assumptions. Not all working women will have children during their work lives. Each pregnancy represents a unique and unpredictable experience for each working woman who has a biological child, and each family adjusts differently.

Accepting the uniqueness of the parenting situation rather than relying on personal past experience or statistical averages is the key to treating working women with dignity. Allowing women the dignity of defining their parenting role within their employers' organizational requirements eliminates the many facets of pregnancy discrimination before, during, and after pregnancy.

Notes

1. Kristen Smith, Barbara Downs, and Martin O'Connell, *Maternity Leave and Employment Patterns: 1961–1995*, Current Population Reports, U.S. Census Bureau.

2. Barbara Downs, *Fertility of American Women: June 2002*, Current Population Reports, U.S. Census Bureau.

3. Ibid.

4. Ibid.

5. The Civil Rights Act of 1964 (known as Title VII) established the EEOC. This federal administrative agency enforces the federal statutes prohibiting employment discrimination.

6. Pregnancy Discrimination Charges EEOC and FEPAs Combined: FY 1992–FY 2004, U.S. Equal Employment Opportunity Commission.

7. *Women at Work: Looking behind the Numbers 40 Years after the Civil Rights Act of 1964*, National Partnership for Women and Families (July 2004).

8. Smith et al., *Maternity Leave and Employment Patterns*.

9. Ibid.

10. See, for example, *Venturelli v. ARC Comm. Servs., Inc.*, 350 F.3d 592 (7th Cir. 2003).

11. EEOC, available online at www.eeoc.gov/types/pregnancy.

12. See Julie Manning Magid, "Contraception and Contractions: A Divergent Decade Following Johnson Controls," *American Business Law Journal* 41 (2003): 115.

13. *Back v. Hastings on Hudson Union Free Sch. Dist.*, 365 F.3d 107, 115 (2004).

14. *Nev. Dep't of Human Res. v. Hibbs*, 538 U.S. 721, 738 (2003).

15. *Back v. Hastings on Hudson*, 121.

16. 42 U.S.C. § 2000e. Title VII regulates the conduct of employers with fifteen or more employees. However, smaller employees typically are covered under similar state legislation prohibiting employment discrimination.

17. "The Civil Rights Act of 1964 was the culmination of decades of debate and political maneuvering over various civil rights proposals. In the end, it took three momentous events to finally propel the bill to the top of the agenda of Congress and the Administration. The first was the August 1963 march on Washington during which Dr. Martin Luther King, Jr., gave his famous 'I have a dream' speech. The second was the September 1963 bombing of a black church in Birmingham, Alabama, in which four little girls were killed. The third was the assassination of President Kennedy, whose support for the bill carried even more weight in Congress and with the public after his untimely death. It was in this time that Bob Dylan warned, 'Come Senators, Congressmen, please heed the call. Don't stand in the doorway, don't block up the hall,' Bob Dylan, The Times They Are A-Changin', on The Times They Are A-Changin' (Sony Music Entertainment/Columbia Records 1964). After months of debate and a seventy-five day filibuster in the Senate, the bill finally passed and was

signed into law by President Johnson on July 2, 1964." *Erickson v. Bartell Drug Co.*, 141 F.Supp. 2d 1266, 1269 n. 4 (W.D. Wash. 2001).

18. Francis J. Vass, *Title VII: Legislative History, Boston College Industrial and Commercial Law Review* 7 (1966): 431.

19. *Gen. Elec. v. Gilbert*, 429 U.S. 125, 143 (1976).

20. Ibid., 136.

21. *Geduldig v. Aiello*, 417 U.S. 484 (1974).

22. *Gen. Elec. v. Gilbert*, 149.

23. Ibid., 161 n. 5.

24. 42 U.S.C. § 2000e(k).

25. H.R. Rep. No. 948, 95th Cong., 2d Sess. at 3 (1978), 1978 U.S. Code Cong. & Ad. News at 4751.

26. See Julie Manning Magid, "Pregnant with Possibility: Reexamining the Pregnancy Discrimination Act," *American Business Law Journal* 38 (2001): 819.

27. *Newport News Shipbuilding & Dry Dock Co. v. EEOC*, 462 U.S. 669, 679 (1983).

28. *Cal. Fed. Sav. & Loan Ass'n. v. Guerra*, 479 U.S. 272 (1987).

29. Ibid., 272, 288–89.

30. *UAW v. Johnson Controls*, 499 U.S. 187 (1991).

31. Ibid., 187, 191–92.

32. *UAW v. Johnson Controls*, 886 F.2d 871, 920 (7th Cir. 1989).

33. *UAW v. Johnson Controls*, 499 U.S. 187, 199 (1991).

34. Ibid., 187, 211.

35. *Erickson v. Bartell Drug Co.*, 141 F.Supp. 2d 1266, 1270 (W.D. Wash. 2001).

36. *Troupe v. May Dep't. Store*, 20 F.3d 734, 738 (7th Cir. 1994).

37. Ann C. McGinley and Jeffrey W. Stempel, "Condescending Contradictions: Richard Posner's Pragmatism and Pregnancy Discrimination," *Florida Law Review* 46 (1994): 193, 210 n. 166.

38. *Troupe v. May Dep't. Store*, 734, 738.

39. *In re Carnegie Ctr. Assocs.*, 129 F.3d 290, 304 (3rd Cir. 1997).

40. *Barrash v. Bowen*, 846 F.2d 927 931-32 (4th Cir. 1988).

41. *EEOC v. Elgin Teachers Assoc.*, 27 F.3d 292, 295 (7th Cir. 1994).

42. *Abraham v. Graphic Arts Int'l Union*, 660 F.2d 811, 819 (D.C. Cir. 1981).

43. *Smith v. F.W. Morse & Co., Inc.*, 76 F.3d 413,424 (1st Cir. 1996).

44. *Maldonado v. U.S. Bank*, 186 F.3d 759, 767 (7th Cir. 1999).

45. "Adverse action" in employment law is any change in employment status that negatively impacts the employee. Such actions include demotion, discipline, termination, changes in job responsibilities, and negative evaluations.

46. *Maldonado v. U.S. Bank*, 759, 767.

47. Ibid.

48. Ibid.

49. 123 Cong. Rec. 29658 (daily ed. Sept. 16, 1977).

50. 124 Cong. Rec. 21442 (1978).

51. 29 U.S.C. § 2601.

52. The Parental and Medical Leave Act of 1986: Joint Hearing before the Subcommittee on Labor-Management Relations and the Subcommittee on Labor Standards of the House Committee on Education and Labor, 99th Cong., 2nd Sess., 100 (1986).

53. 29 CFR § 825.114 (e). "Absences attributable to incapacity [due to pregnancy or for prenatal care] qualify for FMLA leave even though the employee...does not

receive treatment from the health care provider during the absence....[For example, an] employee who is pregnant may be unable to report to work because of severe morning sickness."

54. *Nev. Dep't of Human Res. v. Hibbs*, 721, 737.

55. Ibid., 721.

56. *Erickson v. Bartell Drug Co.*, 1266.

57. Ibid., 1266, 1269.

58. Ibid., 1266, 1274.

59. *Decision on Coverage of Contraception*, EEOC Report, available online at www . eeoc.gov/docs/decision-contraception.

60. Susan A. Cohen, "Federal Law Urged as Culmination of Contraceptive Insurance Coverage Campaign," *Guttmacher Report* 4(5) (October 2001).

61. ERISA, 29 U.S.C. 1144(b)(2)(B).

62. *Dormeyer v. Comerica Bank*, No. 96 C 4805, 1998 U.S. Dist. LEXIS 16585, at *28–29 (N.D. Ill. 1998).

63. *Venturelli v. ARC Comm. Servs., Inc.*, 592.

64. Ibid., 592, 604.

65. *Ilhardt v. Sara Lee Corp.*, 118 F.3d 1151, 1156 (7th Cir. 1997).

66. *Briody v. Am. Gen. Fin. Co.*, No. 98-2728, 1999 U.S. Dist. LEXIS 8405, at *9 (E.D. Pa. May 27, 1999).

67. H.R. Rep. No. 948, 95th Cong., 2d Sess. 3 (1978).

CHAPTER 6

Finding and Keeping the Best and Brightest—Flexible Policies in a Small Workplace

Cristine Cioffi

Managing a small business is a continual tightrope act, with the business owner as the circus master. Finding the balance among incoming work, timely output of product, and the right number and mix of performers to do the job is an art form. Strike the right balance, and the performance is magical; one missed step on the high-wire, and the entire act tumbles. This case study of a small law firm will offer workplace employment policies designed to encourage and support the performers (your employees) in a sure-footed and dazzling performance.

The Law Firm

The business is a New York law firm established in the format of a professional corporation (Cioffi • Slezak • Wildgrube, P.C.; www.cswlawfirm.com hereafter referred to as "CSW"). There are three shareholders, or owners, of the firm, which was founded twelve years ago. Two are part-time partners; one is full time. All references to "partners" technically refer to shareholders of the firm.

To put the part-time partner issue in context, in the upstate New York legal community, for a shareholder, or partner, of a law practice to work less than 100 percent of a workweek is a radical departure from the norm. Traditional business models for law firms require the owners of the firms to work at least a full-time schedule. The New York State Bar Association Committee on Women in the Law has surveyed and researched the needs of women practitioners and has concluded that women attorneys throughout New York State are looking for firms that will allow them to have management responsibility on a part-time work schedule.[1,2] CSW's experience has been a true win/win situation, but it has not been replicated by many firms.

Staffing levels at the firm fluctuate. Presently there are two full-time associate attorneys, three part-time paralegals, three full-time paralegals, two receptionists who job share, and a part-time bookkeeper. Part-time staff work three to five days per week and some part-time staff work an abbreviated day. The firm frequently employs a law clerk, usually a law student, who researches issues on an hourly basis. Coincidentally, all of the attorney and nonattorney staff currently employed are women.

What Motivated the Formation of the Firm?

The firm was founded in 1995 in an effort to create a more sympathetic workplace for women. Two of the current partners at CSW were trained in larger, traditional firms, intolerant of part-time attorneys. Each came from a firm having little to no experience with attorney maternity leaves.

Barriers that were unique to women attorneys in the 1980s included physical challenges: carrying thirty pounds of files into a courthouse while pregnant; finding a private space to express breast milk during the workday; reporting to work daily while chronically sleep deprived. In an era in which male partners ground out billable hours during the day and courted clients at night in the name of business development, the pregnant or postpartum attorney was seen as shirking her duty and thus placed at a distinct disadvantage relative to her male peers.

Of the two partners who were groomed in this environment, each woman met with resistance to her attempts to change business practices within the existing firm structures. CSW was launched on the premise that "family comes first" and that the solution to full coverage of all client matters could be found in teamwork. The firm was conceived on the principle that women attorneys could concurrently have satisfying family and professional lives, without sacrificing quality in their legal work.

The Bigger Picture

In the United States, women composed half of the workforce by the late 1990s. By the year 2000, almost 77 percent of *all* women worked outside the home (Halpern, 2005). In 2007, women-owned businesses employ 27.5 million workers and generate receipts of $3.6 trillion.[3] The number of firms owned at least 50 percent by women expanded their number of employees by 28 percent between 1997 and 2005, which was three times the growth rate of all firms with employees.[4] These facts demonstrate a shift in the U.S. workforce, with women playing larger roles.

Currently, many women work through a full-term pregnancy, and many are back at their jobs even sooner than the legal disability period accorded a postpartum woman by New York State law (New York State Labor Law

§206-b). Economic necessity drives many women to return to employment prematurely. In contemporary culture, more women than men organize their family's child care and accept household management responsibility. Many employed women become caretakers for elderly parents, or a disabled sibling. Added responsibilities for family place an extraordinary burden on working women. Businesses have begun to step forward to accommodate this segment of the workforce, and CSW was developed in an effort to offer women in the legal profession a supportive environment in which to practice.

An Ethic of Care

In 1995, the founding partners of the firm (initially incorporated as "Carpenter & Cioffi, PC") joined in an effort to create a workplace that reflected sound family values and the belief that quality legal services could be provided in a "nontraditional" workplace. The goal was to create a workplace founded on an "ethic of care." The phrase, published ten years after the founding of the firm, comes from Ruth O'Brien in *Bodies in Revolt* (O'Brien, 2005). In that work, she describes the balancing of the needs of the business versus the needs of the employees. She traces the concept of the care ethic to Carol Gilligan's work (1982).

An ethic of care recognizes the differences between people and that it is incumbent on the moral employer to meet the needs of its workforce. Employee needs vary. Consider a 23-year-old staffer (no kids, thinking of grad school, and dating a hot guy); a 38-year-old partner (surrounded by diapers and Fisher-Price toys, while driving from work to two day care providers); and a 53-year-old partner (grown children and aging parents). Each faces different challenges in both home life and professional life. Each person is valued in the workplace, and each contributes uniquely. Policies of the workplace must be flexible enough to allow each of these workers to balance personal and family needs with her career.

In a workplace founded on an ethic of care, both employer and employee are permitted, indeed encouraged, to overtly acknowledge that their families (not their jobs) are their highest priority. No one need feign an illness to attend a child's parent-teacher conference nor feel guilt over accompanying an elderly parent to a doctor's appointment. The workplace is steeped in the care ethic. The firm acknowledges the importance and validity of these responsibilities and takes steps to accommodate the worker's absence.

A Statement of the Firm's Philosophy

At CSW, each interview begins with a statement of the philosophy of the firm. It might sound like this: "We want your full attention while you're here, but your family comes first. We will give you six personal days and two weeks vacation for you to use as you need to. If you have kids, we expect you to be at every parent-teacher conference. If you've got a sick parent, take time to transport him or her to the doctor. We have a liberal 'makeup' policy—that is, if you only need to be out for ninety minutes, you are free to make up that time during the two-week pay period, so you don't diminish your personal and vacation days."

Originally, the firm distinguished between sick and personal days. It became quickly apparent that the purpose of the employee's absence was of no consequence to the partners, and all days were converted to personal days. The next segment of the applicant interview addresses the kind of reciprocity the firm expects from an employee. It is explained to the applicant that he or she will be part of a team. If an employee needs to rush out of the office to pick up a sick child at school, another staff member or attorney will pick up the client work and keep the file moving forward. In turn, each employee must be willing to cover additional duties when other staff have urgent family or personal needs. In most instances, this transition between staff is invisible to the client. The care ethic recognizes that all members of the firm are both care givers and care receivers.

In the course of the twelve-year experience of CSW, members of the firm have seen all the ups and downs life has to offer: attorneys and staff alike have been through the death of a parent; the birth and adoption of children; children who needed surgery; staff themselves who have needed surgery. The firm has celebrated weddings. Co-workers have survived the turmoils of life with teenagers. Each member of the firm knows that family is more important than a job and that if co-workers help each other, everyone can be very good at both.

Combining an ethic of care with a team work style has engendered incredible loyalty to the firm. Staff share and appreciate the values on which the firm is founded and the partners' respect for their family lives. They accept responsibility for getting the work done; they take the initiative to complete unfinished work. They rally behind each other in a crisis.

In 2001, the firm won the first Carol S. Knox Family-Friendly Award given by the Capital District Women's Bar Association. The best part of the award was that the firm was nominated by a staff member.

Is Business Success Possible with Family-Friendly Policies?

Consider the issue of profitability. Can a law firm be family friendly and still make money? Happily, the answer is yes. Partners continually reevaluate staff pay scales to remain competitive from a salary perspective. Annual revenues have increased. The firm has grown from five employees in 1995 to a payroll of fifteen employees today. In October 2006, CSW was named "Enterprise of the Year" by the Chamber of Schenectady County. The award recognized one business in the county for growth and good management. Of course, success is measured in more than just numbers. The firm has a stable team of staff members who take pride and pleasure in their workplace.

Work Flow and the Staff Characteristics Needed to Sustain It

At CSW, file work flows down and out, as though poured from the top of a pyramid. It is the role of the partners to attract clients, bring legal work in-house, evaluate what needs to be done, and do the portions of it that require the legal expertise of a partner. Associates and paralegal staff are then able to leverage partner production. The balance of the work flows down the pyramid to the lowest paid person on staff who can competently handle each task. Work for each client is often divided among staff members. Using an estate planning matter as an example, the partner will meet with the client and identify the trusts, transfers, etc. necessary to attain the client's objective. The partner may then assign one paralegal to run estate tax or income tax projections of the plan, another staff person to prepare deeds to fund into a trust, and a third staff person to prepare a draft of the trust itself. The partner supervises, making sure there is communication between each staff person. It is the partner's responsibility to proofread and revise and, when the project is ready, to meet with the client and present a draft estate plan.

A firm handling complex matters needs to recruit a sophisticated staff. Not only do staff need to have the substantive skills and intellect to do the job (estate administration, real estate, and corporate matters), but they need to be bright enough, flexible, and cooperative enough to be a contributing member of the firm team. CSW functions well only if staff are willing to take initiative, secure enough to take risks in the workplace, and are mature enough to work well with others who may have different skill sets.

The work of a law firm is that of processing technical information in a manner that is coherent to the client and technically proficient in the professional setting, be it courtroom, IRS office, real estate closing table, etc. It depends on all workers embracing cooperation, teamwork, and worker's autonomy and responsibility. These are all characteristics described by Manuel Castells (1996). To create this magic formula, the employer must deliberately cultivate a cooperative and productive workplace culture. This type of work is empowered by a computer network and e-mail communications. The ability of each staff member to research electronically keeps the firm's knowledge base current and contributes to the quality of the work product.

The Culture of the Workplace

As a workplace, CSW is very relational. With this work model, it is next to impossible for any staff member to remain isolated. As people work together, they talk. All the observations that Louise Lamphere (1985) identified are true in the CSW workplace. The current (female) staff bond as wives, mothers, and sisters. Workers discuss health issues, aging issues, books, movies, and TV shows. The firm celebrates together: birthdays, engagements, graduations, and weddings. Staff members attend funerals and cry together. Firm members eat together—almost continuously. Regularly scheduled staff meetings occur every four weeks, and individuals rotate responsibility for taking minutes, chairing the meeting, or procuring lunch. Staff meetings provide an opportunity for any staff member to impact the workplace, in a nonthreatening atmosphere.

By working in a team, co-workers learn each other's vulnerabilities and strengths. Staff learn to trust each other. Workers who cannot be trusted are terminated. Firm members respect each other's knowledge and have respect for each other's differences.

Off-site activities provide other ways for staff to collaborate. One firm retreat was held at our local Girls Incorporated. It was a day of team problem solving, eating, and mastering the high ropes course. Each participant learned more about her co-workers, in a setting completely foreign to the practice of law. Bowling is another firm activity that creates a team dynamic different from that in the office. Who would know that the quietest paralegal on staff can bowl a score of 162?

The firm also has a culture of productivity. Focus is important: the completion of the clients' legal work is what allows each member of the firm, collectively, to earn a living. CSW uses a computerized time and billing system called "TABS." It requires each staff person (attorney and nonattorney) to enter all of her time spent each day into a variety of categories such as client files, firm administration, or business development. Reports can then be generated that can guide business management. For example, partners can observe how much time each employee spent on client files, what revenues were generated from this work, and what areas of work are most productive (e.g., real estate, business and corporate, or trust and estate)?

Originally, this information was reviewed only by partners. It provided data to develop budgets, spot trends, and address understaffed areas. Last year, partners began giving each employee her own weekly report of hours worked. Partners were very discrete and counseled workers individually if someone was having trouble with timekeeping, or was falling behind in production. Shortly after initiating this change, however, it was inadvertently discovered that staff were rushing to compare their weekly reports with each other and that good-natured competitions had developed to see who had more billable hours. It was a sign to partners that staff understood the purpose of the record keeping and did not feel threatened. Really, it was a sign of success in building toward a common purpose. Partners are now beginning to share more quantitative data with staff, on a selected basis.

The lesson learned is that the more economic information that is shared with staff, the more engaged they become in meeting financial goals. Staff take pride in results that can be measured. Staff have recognized that there is greater productivity in team efforts. In a way, it has shifted the sense of responsibility from partners only to partners and staff.

A Horizontal Management Model

One outcome of the business practices and policies developed at CSW is a shift from a vertical model of management—the one utilized at the traditional firms of the 1980s, where senior attorneys controlled every aspect of the firm —to a horizontal management model, where staff have a voice in setting goals and policies, controlling the flow of the workplace, and are given information about outcomes. The experience at CSW has been that the more highly engaged worker cares more about her work product, is more willing to support the work of co-workers, and is more productive. A summary of the policies and practices of CSW follows:

1. *Part-time employment.* One of the commodities people value as much as money is time. CSW has encountered a range of reasons why workers want part-time employment: a second job; a long-term illness that can be controlled with a four-day-per-week schedule, but cannot be managed with full-time employment; the need to devote important time to children. Part-time employment options have been extended to partners as well as other staff.

2. *Flextime.* Some staff are early birds who just like to come in at 7:30 A.M.; others are parents who need to meet the school bus at 2:30 P.M. The firm is willing to accommodate these schedules, with the mutual expectation that all assigned work will be completed in a timely fashion. Special care is extended to train staff to make both part-time and flextime positions invisible to clients. Clients are accepting of these policies, as long as their needs are being met.

3. *Desk sharing.* Having both part-time and flextime employees has allowed the firm to use the same physical desk space for two employees, a practice called "hot desking." Partners coordinate the hours that each employee will be in the office, so she knows she has a desk and a computer for her workday. Desk mates have been willing to accept responsibility for these arrangements. It puts employees in control of their own schedules.

4. *Maternity-leave policies.* Through both births and adoptions the firm remains flexible regarding maternity leaves. Considerations are given to each individual, and a leave is tailored to meet her needs. As examples, the firm has offered part-time status to returning mothers, as well as the ability to work from home one or two days per week.

5. *Breast-feeding policies.* New moms are encouraged to bring their breast pumps to work. By using a particular "Do Not Disturb" sign on the office door, all staff know not to interrupt the process until the sign is removed. Attorneys have been known to answer e-mail and phone calls while pumping.

6. *Off-site work.* When a long-term staff member announced that her partner was moving to Florida and she would like to go with him, the firm developed a plan with her in which the firm provided her with computer equipment, a toll-free phone number, and a Federal Express account. She handled estate administration files from her remote location, shipping hard copies of documents as needed. With improvements in scanning technology, this could now be done without moving as much actual paper as in the past.

7. *Job sharing.* The reception staff at CSW has consisted of two people filling one position for a few years now. One woman has chosen to volunteer time at a local not-for-profit two days per week. The other is a trained executive secretary who came out of retirement to work two days per week. Their job-share techniques are seamless. The needs of the firm are met, as are the needs of the employees involved.

8. *401(k) with profit sharing.* A 401(k) plan had been established in 1995, when the firm opened. But as the setting of economic goals became more of a team process, partners decided that another tangible indicator of the firm's success would be to have staff participate in a profit-sharing plan. A second issue developed with the 401(k) plan when the plan administrator originally selected by the partners left the business; it became necessary to find a new plan administrator. A committee of three (nonpartner) staff members was named to interview new administrators and make a recommendation to the firm.

9. *Performance reviews.* Partners conduct an initial performance review after three months of employment, annual reviews thereafter. Reviews are conducted separately from salary raises to encourage candor from both employer and employee. The staff likes feedback. A three-month review gives partners an opportunity to counsel a new staff member on both work quality and work process. The team setting is an integrative experience, and many employees have not worked this way before. The performance appraisal measurement tool is a document completed by both attorneys and the person being reviewed, in advance of the meeting date. Two partners then meet with the staff person to share respective observations and set goals for the employee for the next twelve months. All employees except the three partners are "at will" employees.

10. *Health insurance.* In the 2007 workplace this is a "hot button" issue. CSW has chosen to provide each employee with individual health care coverage through the Chamber of Schenectady County. Employees can then supplement this to privately pay for family coverage. Although this is an expensive benefit, partners have agreed that it is an important way to convey concern for employee needs.

11. *Monthly staff meetings.* A schedule of meetings is set for the year, alternating between Tuesdays and Thursdays, to accommodate part-time staff. Agenda items are sought in advance from everyone. Each meeting has a facilitator, a reporter, and a food procurer. Every attorney and staff person takes a turn in each role. Apart from encouraging the full flow of information within the firm, it has been gratifying to watch some of the staff attain the level of self-confidence needed to chair a meeting. Each person contributes. One of the norms observed is that no one will be disparaged for an opinion that is not shared by others.

12. *Mentoring.* The firm provides a mentor for each new employee. An associate attorney or law clerk is mentored by a partner. A new paralegal may be mentored by an experienced paralegal. It is a way to continue the training and integration of each person into the firm. It also provides a new employee with a personal "link" into the firm network. New staff have someone to ask questions of, without risking embarrassment or criticism.

13. *Wellness.* In an effort to promote physical health, the firm has offered to reimburse employees' co-pays for an annual physical. In addition, and as an incentive, the

firm gives each employee who has an annual physical a gift certificate for a one-hour massage.

What Does the Future Hold?

The practice of law has seen many evolutions in the last three decades. Attorneys no longer dictate to secretaries, carbon paper is gone, print libraries are disappearing, "paperless" offices are springing into place, and electronic possibilities for communication and research expand daily. There is no reason to doubt that this rocket-like propulsion will continue and that tomorrow and next month and next year law firms will be contemplating new ways to do business and better ways to provide quality legal services to clients.

To survive in the future, small businesses of every nature will need to remain open to change, at both the staff and management levels. Change can be difficult for both employer and employee. It will be the role of management as the "ringmaster" of this circus to identify the next generation of workplace impediments for staff. Business managers will then need to develop policies and practices to overcome such hurdles and to keep their acrobats (employees) "limber." It is the responsibility of management to keep staff engaged and educated, prepared to develop positive change from within. In this manner, whether managing a circus performance or a law firm, a competent, professional performance is assured.

Notes

1. New York State Bar Association Committee on Women in the Law.
2. Gender Equity in the Legal Profession; May 2002.
3. U.S. Department of Labor, *Women's Bureau Trends and Challenges for Work in the 21st Century*, http://www.choose2lead.org/Publications/Many%20Faces%20of%2021st%20Century%20Working%20Women.pdf.
4. Center for Women's Business Research, *Top Facts About Women-Owned Businesses*, http://www.womensbusinessresearch.org/content/index.php?pid=45.

Selected Bibliography

Castells, M. (1996). *The rise of the network society*. New York: Blackwell.
Gilligan, C. (1982). *In a different voice: Psychological theory and women's development*. Cambridge, MA: Harvard University Press.
Halpern, D. (2005). Psychology at the intersection of work and family: Recommendations for employers, working families, and policymakers. *American Psychologist, 60,* 397–409.
Lamphere, L. (1985). Bringing the family to work: Women's culture on the shop floor. *Feminist Studies, 11,* 519–540.
O'Brien, R. (2005). *Bodies in revolt: Gender, disability and a work ethic of care*. New York: Routledge.

CHAPTER 7

Career Paths and Family in the Academy: Progress and Challenges

Bianca L. Bernstein and Nancy Felipe Russo

Virtually every study and report on women in institutions of higher education documents the difficulties women face in balancing the demands of academic work and family responsibilities (e.g., Committee on Maximizing the Potential of Women in Academic Science and Engineering [CMPWASE], et al., 2006; National Research Council, 2001; National Science Foundation [NSF], 2004, 2007). The problems are severe. For example, in a National Research Council (NRC) study of female engineering faculty, by far the most important factor reported as having a negative impact, identified by 52 percent of respondents, was "balancing work and family responsibilities" (NRC, 2001).

Recent efforts to introduce family-friendly policies for academic employees are a positive development to ameliorate these difficulties. In this chapter, we review work and family issues in the academy and the policy and program initiatives that are being developed to address them. In the process, we examine the relationship between career and family conflict and women's career paths and well-being. We argue that the failure by institutions and individuals to adequately address work/family conflict issues and provide better means for integrating academic work and family responsibilities has serious and permanent effects on academic women's lives. We view graduate school as a formative period in which female graduate students acquire their views on whether and how it is possible to lead a balanced and integrated life in the academy. These views in turn play a pivotal role in determining how work and family issues are conceptualized and dealt with over the life course, with initial choices serving as powerful determinants of options that are available in later years. Finally, we offer a set of approaches to enhance women's success in integrating academic careers and family.

Women in the Academy: Still Underrepresented

As we explore the issues that women face in the academy, we draw the distinction between "work" and "career." We borrow from the Vandewater, Ostrove, and Stewart (1997) definitions of careers ("work requiring advanced education and having a clear ladder of advancement") and jobs ("work requiring little or no advanced education and having no clear ladder of advancement") (p. 1150). We select the term "career" for examining women in academic life, and specifically for faculty and graduate students in Ph.D. programs, because it is most fitting for describing the vocational roles of people with status, achievement, and relative affluence (Blustein, 2006; Richardson, 1993).

While there are reports of increases in the numbers of women in faculty and administrative positions in U.S. universities and colleges, women's gains in status are neither consistent nor universal. The proportion of female doctoral recipients has increased, but the representation of women faculty has not reflected these gains. Faculty continue to be predominately white and male, and among men and women who hold science and engineering doctorates, four times as many men as women hold full-time faculty positions (CMPWASE, et al., 2006). Whereas women comprise almost half of the faculty at two-year colleges and almost four out of ten teaching faculty positions at baccalaureate-granting institutions, they are fewer than 30 percent of all professors teaching in the high prestige research institutions in the United States. Women faculty are better represented in the humanities, social sciences, and education, compared to the sciences, engineering, and business, where they are scarce.

The underrepresentation of ethnic minority women among university faculty is of particular concern, and therefore the low number of women from underrepresented groups who earn Ph.D.s and comprise the eligibility pool for faculty openings is even more pressing. Using NSF labels, of doctorates awarded in 2001 to women who were U.S. citizens or permanent residents, 69 percent went to whites, 14 percent to Asians, 10 percent to blacks, and—of most relevance to the Southwest—9 percent to Hispanics. Fewer than 1 percent went to American Indian/Alaskan Natives (NSF, 2004).

Indeed, despite the national spotlight on these issues generated by the 1999 report criticizing Massachusetts Institute of Technology's (MIT) treatment of women faculty in science, the percentage of women scientists at MIT actually dropped in all departments other than chemistry and physics. A report on gender equity by the American Association of University Professors (2006) indicates that the proportions of women who hold tenure-line positions (44.8 percent), tenured positions (31 percent), faculty positions at the full professor rank (24 percent), and middle and upper level positions in academic administration are still far below the proportions of women with doctoral degrees and the proportions of men in comparable positions, even when looking across all types of higher education institutions and in fields where there are similar proportions of eligible men and women. Salary differentials continue as well, with female professors earning 81 percent of what men earn across all ranks and types of institutions in 2005–2006 (American Association of University Professors [AAUP], 2006).

The attrition of talented women from the academy begins early on and continues at each successive step, even after professional goals emerge and women consider graduate programs. The drop in numbers of women is quite dramatic, from undergraduate majors (60 percent of U.S. undergraduates are now women), to graduate majors, to graduate degrees, to assistant professor, through to full professor, and to leadership positions in higher education. Even where enrollments and numbers of degrees granted to women have increased, the low numbers and downward spiral are still apparent. For example, in engineering, there was a 35-fold increase in the proportion of Ph.D.s granted to women in engineering from 1970 to 2004, but the proportion is still only at 15 percent (Committee on Professionals in Science and Technology, 2006), as seen in Table 7.1. One snapshot of the trends in the sciences and engineering (see Table 7.1) was provided by Jo Handelsman and her colleagues (2005) based on data from Donna Nelson's work (2005) and NSF's Survey of Earned Doctorates:

Researchers have attributed the differential representation of men and women in the tenure-track and tenured faculty in the academy to a range of factors. In an important statement to the scientific community about the relative paucity of faculty women in science, Handelsman and her colleagues (2005) pointed to barriers such as pipeline losses, campus climates that are

Table 7.1
Women Ph.D.s and Faculty, Top 50 Departments in Selected Disciplines*

Discipline (% women)		Career level (% women)		
	Ph.D.	Asst. Professor	Assoc. Professor	Full Professor
Biology	45.89	30.20	24.87	14.79
Physical Science	24.68	16.13	14.18	6.36
Astronomy	22.88	20.18	15.69	9.75
Chemistry	33.42	21.47	20.50	7.62
Computer Science	15.27	10.82	14.41	8.33
Math & Statistics	26.90	19.60	13.19	4.56
Physics	14.78	11.15	9.41	5.24
Engineering	15.34	16.94	11.17	3.68
Electrical	12.13	10.86	9.84	3.85
Civil	17.90	22.26	11.50	3.52
Mechanical	10.93	15.65	8.89	3.17
Chemical	24.98	21.38	19.19	4.37

*Data on Ph.D.s and faculty come from the same "Top 50" departments for each discipline; departments are ranked by NSF according to research expenditures in that discipline.

chilly for women, unconscious bias among evaluators of scholarship, promotion, and tenure records, and work and family balance. The lack of sponsorship and collegial networks has also been cited as a significant contributor to the dearth of women in the academy. Some of these challenges have been referred to as the "glass ceiling," denoting the often invisible forces that restrict women's advancement.

The accumulation of disadvantages, barriers, and challenges that many women face is so daunting that Cole (1979) referred to the women who persevered and defied the odds to become faculty as "survivors." For those who would imagine that those survivors had an easier path, there is considerable evidence to the contrary. Several studies (e.g., Clark & Corcoran, 1986) and biographies and autobiographies of countless women faculty with records of distinction (e.g., Daniell, 2006; O'Connell & Russo, 1983, 1988; Pritchard, 2006) reveal the difficulties they experienced with advisors and colleagues, inadequate mentoring and sponsorship, exclusion and isolation, and multiple role demands of work and family. Tracing the ways in which these women resisted or overcame these disadvantages is an important area of study that can inform the women who face them still today.

It is important to note that while advancement in the representation of women in ranked faculty positions continues to lag, the number of women in untenured and part-time academic positions continues to swell. Multiple studies have demonstrated that the concentration of women in the lower-paid, lower-prestige, part-time, and temporary teaching positions is due, in large part, to the conflicts between career and family demands. For women, as Bronstein and colleagues put it so aptly, "having both a family and an academic career is no simple matter. The tenure system in the United States was set up for male faculty, whose wives provided all the homemaking so that their husbands could devote their energies solely to academic career advancement" (Bronstein, Rothblum, & Solomon, 1993).

There is a developing awareness that career outcomes derive from the accumulation of slight advantages that favor men and slight inequities that disadvantage women (e.g., CMPWASE, et al., 2006; Valian, 1999), but there is insufficient translation of how these inequities operate in particular academic and disciplinary contexts. A number of scholars have pointed to the gendered nature of science and of academic institutions. Lotte Bailyn (2003) articulately summarizes the implications of such research: "What this means is that the academy is anchored in assumptions about competence and success that have led to practices and norms constructed around the life experiences of men, and around a vision of masculinity as the normal, universal requirement of university life" (p. 143). She points to questions that have been raised about academic culture, such as whether the fully autonomous expert role is a necessary condition for first-rate scholarship and whether success requires total priority given to one's work, and reminds us how easy it is to forget that venerable academic practices, such as the tenure clock, are "not God-given, but are constructed by mere men" (p. 143).

For purposes of this analysis, we start with the recognition that while women do encounter troubling forces and severe academic challenges, of most concern are the talented women who are well positioned to meet those academic challenges but still elect to drop off the "fast track." Instead, they choose less pressured positions or life alternatives that do not provide the full range of stimulation and opportunity for which they had prepared.

We emphasize that people's choices are rarely unconstrained or made in a neutral social context. To understand this concept, one need only imagine what men would decide about careers if they were expected to be the primary caretakers for their children (Valian, 2007). In finding that 85 percent of the more than thirty highly educated and accomplished brides whose wedding announcements appeared in the January 1996 *New York Times* had left the workplace in whole or in part after having babies, Hirshman (2006) resoundingly rejects the concept of "choice feminism." She writes,

> These were the girls who were going to make their lives from their wits and their brains, not their looks, trust funds, and reproductive organs. Immensely desirable mates, they should have been able to find spouses whose needs would not require, overtly or covertly, that they quit their jobs. (p. 24)

In a society where it is assumed and often demonstrated that having a high-octane professional career and enjoying a rich family life are incompatible, women view their options as limited. As Geraldine Richards, a chemist at the University of Oregon and leader of the Committee on the Advancement of Women Chemists organization, observed, "Women are scared away because they don't see how they can put together a life that satisfies their personal and professional goals. They see that the best jobs are obtained by people who want to only do science and give it 100 percent" (Wilson, 2004). In study after study, researchers find that balancing career and family stands out as an overwhelming difficulty faced by academic women, particularly those in science and engineering (e.g., Rosser, 2004). It is the role of the family in juxtaposition to the promise of academic work that we explore here as a major contributor to a woman's decision to "opt out."

Women Graduate Students

In the early 1970s, women earned only 16 percent of all the Ph.D.s awarded in the United States. Thirty-five years later, women received over 50 percent of the Ph.D.s awarded to Americans. The distribution among fields is disparate, however, with the highest proportions of doctoral degrees going to women in the humanities, social sciences, and education. In the physical science and engineering fields, the proportion of Ph.D.s awarded to women ranges from as low as 11 percent to a high of 27 percent, with the exception of chemistry where one of three Ph.D.s goes to women (see Table 7.1 from Handelsman, et al., 2005, on p. 91).

Not only is the proportion of women earning Ph.D.s still low, but there is now growing recognition that fewer women complete their Ph.D. programs than those who enroll in these programs. That is, there is a significant rate of attrition among all doctoral students (completion rates are estimated at 57 percent across all fields) (Danecke, 2005; Frasier, 2006; Nevill & Chen, 2007). Completion rates vary by field: 54.7 percent in math and physical sciences and 64.4 percent in engineering (Frasier, 2006). And while the attrition rate is lower in the physical sciences and engineering when compared to the humanities, preliminary data (Danecke, 2005; Frasier, 2006) confirm the earlier findings that the attrition rates among women doctoral students in these fields are higher than those of their male peers (e.g., Berg & Ferber, 1983; Nerad & Cerny, 1999; Zwick, 1991). A study of completion rates at Duke University (Siegel, 2005) also found significantly lower Ph.D. completion rates in the biological sciences for women (67 percent) than for men (76 percent).

Accurate figures for the attrition (or Ph.D. completion) gap between men and women are not available and cannot be derived from existing data available from the National Science Foundation because these data are neither longitudinal nor disaggregated by masters versus doctoral student enrollment. The difference between the percentage of women enrolled in doctoral programs and those completing doctoral programs is one (albeit tenuous) way to estimate the gap. For example, while women represent 22 percent of doctoral students enrolled in engineering, they receive only 17 percent of engineering doctorates; in mathematics and the physical sciences, women comprise 32 percent of doctoral students but earn just 24 percent of mathematics and computer science doctorates and 27 percent of those in physical sciences (General Accountability Office [GAO], 2004). The Ph.D. Completion Project, currently under way and guided by the Council of Graduate Schools and supported by Pfizer, Inc. and the Ford Foundation, attempts to overcome the problem of variations in student records and definitions by collecting comparable information about cohorts from universities across the United States. The forthcoming reports will hopefully provide more reliable and disaggregated estimates regarding the magnitude of the gender gap in doctoral attrition by field.

Women's Experiences in Doctoral Programs

With the support of a National Research Foundation grant (Bernstein, Horan, & Anderson-Rowland, 2006), a large project is under way to develop an Internet-based resilience training package that is designed to strengthen the persistence of women in physical science and engineering Ph.D. programs, male-dominated fields where women are most underrepresented. We begin with the notion that an important way to understand the problems of retention in and attrition from graduate programs is through the lens of a single student. Specifically, we take the position that a woman's persistence or attrition represents an act based on one or more decisions, whether considered or ill-considered, in response to her *perceptions* of her present environment *and her predictions about her possible futures.*

Recognizing that people judge their ability to cope with situations (coping self-efficacy; Lent, Brown, & Hackett, 2000) on the basis of their own experiences and observing the experiences of others (vicarious learning; Bandura, 1986, 1997), we consider both what graduate students experience as well as what they observe to be influential in their estimates of future coping. Hence, as a first step in studying and attempting to ameliorate the potential decision of women to leave their Ph.D. programs before completing them, we conducted focus groups with seventy women in Ph.D. programs in the physical sciences, mathematics, and engineering at a major research-extensive university (Bernstein, Russo, & Anderson-Rowland, 2007). We sought to understand what the women students experienced on a daily basis that is either encouraging or discouraging in their progress toward the Ph.D. Two faculty members co-facilitated ten focus groups with women students clustered by subject area, domestic or international status, and interdisciplinary experience. Trained notetakers and audiotapes recorded the participants' responses to seven questions about daily encouragers, discouragers, and advice they would offer to future women doctoral students.

We collected demographic information and responses to two questions about their satisfaction with their Ph.D. program (0–100 percent satisfied) and the likelihood of completing their Ph.D. program (0–100 percent likely). The mean age of the women was 28.32, their mean years in the program was 2.28, 59 percent had a master's degree, 67 percent were married or in a committed relationship, and 20 percent had at least one child. We found a significant positive correlation between satisfaction with the program and probability of completion ($r = 0.38$, $p = 0.004$) and a significant negative correlation between satisfaction with the program and number of years completed in the Ph.D. program ($r = -0.33$, $p = 0.016$).

It is not difficult to imagine that with the "cumulative adversities" that women face as graduate student women in male-dominated science and engineering fields, they might be questioning whether to continue in their programs. As Sonnert and Holton (1995) have written about the impact of many small and subtle disadvantages, "Science careers appeared to be shaped, to a considerable extent, by numerous idiosyncratic events and characteristics that are often insignificant by themselves but become forceful in their accumulation" (p. 123). We reason, therefore, that documenting their phenomenological experience will help us design a program of interventions to combat the impact and reduce the frequency of these adversities or microstressors.

To understand the women's lived experience of encouragement and discouragement in their programs, we used the qualitative approach of psychological phenomenology (Moustakas, 1994; Polkinghorne, 1989). We reduced the large body of data from notes and transcripts of the focus groups to significant statements and quotes, categorized these statements into themes, and developed textual and structural descriptions to capture the essence of what characterizes encouragement and discouragement for our purposeful selection of women in science and engineering.

What was most striking in our analysis was the depth and frequency of discouragement expressed by the women who participated in the focus groups. We were surprised to find that a large number of women, women in each focus group, regardless of disciplinary group or whether domestic or international, expressed considerable discouragement. The extent of discouragement many women feel is recognizable in statements such as the following:

- "I'm questioning if I made good decisions. It's a daily, weekly struggle to continue."
- "You just get broken down. Your will is broken down. Why am I putting myself through this? You go through the motions."
- "I'm very disillusioned with how it all works."
- "Frankly speaking, sometimes I have a hard time to keep going. So I keep questioning it every day whether this is what you want. But now, it is that I want to just push through and finish and then decide. Again, I was not sure right from the beginning that I want to do this. A lot of uncertainties all the time. My plus points are on a low side these days."

We concluded from our careful analysis of all the focus group statements and quotations that there were three principal categories of concerns and discouragers expressed by women participants (Bernstein, Russo, & Anderson-Rowland, 2007). These principal categories had to do with advisors, inhospitable program environments, and career and family conflict issues. To examine whether we identified discouragers that pertain more to women than men, we conducted four additional focus groups using the same methodology with a total of twenty-two domestic and international men from the engineering and computer sciences. Even though both women and men discussed issues they had with their advisors, the women were much more discouraged about the relationship with their advisors than were the men (Anderson-Rowland, Bernstein, & Russo, 2007). Categories of chilly academic climate and career-life conflict were found to be characteristic of primary discouragers reported by the women but not by the men participating in these focus groups.

It was interesting to note several instances when men reported that the challenges they faced with advisors increased their determination to persist. We heard repeatedly from men that they would not ever consider aborting something they had started. In one case, a male doctoral student reported that since his wife had dropped out of the Ph.D. program to stay home with a child, he needed to get the degree for both of them.

The first area of common discouragement for women in the focus groups was associated with disappointments and frustrations with the advisor. The woman's relationship with her advisor was a common complaint. We found the advisor category to comprise three types of difficulties: inadequate feedback and direction from the advisor, a mismatch of working styles and/or expectations for the woman's program work and career goals, and an advisor who was overly critical and demanding.

The second source of women's discouragement can be described generally as a chilly academic climate. The term "chilly climate" was introduced in the 1980s (Hall & Sandler, 1982) to describe the environment women experience in academic settings that contributes to discouragement and lowered self-esteem. Science has been portrayed as inherently masculine in its structure, epistemology, and methodology (e.g., Keller & Longino, 1996). The male-centered culture is characterized by the gendered vocabulary of science (Keller, 1995), a highly competitive environment, and greater tendency for men to promote themselves, and appears to be enacted most in the laboratory setting (Rosser, 2004).

Although overt hostility and discrimination still exist and need to be countered, the concept of chilly climate foreshadowed the recognition that prejudice and discrimination can be expressed in more subtle ways as well. In addition to the competitive and harsh environment that the women in our focus groups reported, we also found two other significant aspects to their chilly climate: their sense of isolation and marginalization and being subjected to gender stereotyping and potential discrimination. We report the results in the categories of issues with advisors and mentors and chilly climate more fully elsewhere (Bernstein, Russo, & Anderson-Rowland, 2007).

One of the things that makes dealing with stereotyped, prejudiced, or discriminatory behaviors in today's academy so difficult is that many of the processes that underlie such behaviors are implicit; that is, they occur beyond conscious awareness (Banji & Greenwald, 1995). Consequently, people who are well-intentioned can nonetheless behave in ways that have harmful effects on a woman's self-confidence and perceived competence. Correcting the behavior of colleagues or mentors without affecting one's interpersonal relationship with them is difficult if not impossible, underscoring the importance of having organizations of graduate and faculty women that can educate faculty about the unintended consequences of their behaviors. Such organizations or social networks can also counter feelings of isolation and marginalization.

We affix the broad label of career-life conflict to the third major source of discouragement for our focus group women in the physical sciences, mathematics, and engineering. Some women in our focus groups specifically pointed to family and happiness as potentially incompatible with their academic pursuits. For example, one woman lamented, "I'm sick of school. I want to get married, have a family, get a house. "Another speculated, "I wonder if it's a woman thing. Maybe the male ego pushes them to finish. For men, it's status. For women that's not important. It is an illusion—I want to be happy."

Previous research suggests that among students who are dissatisfied with their doctoral programs, more women (58 percent) than men (47 percent) perceive their department's lack of support for work/life balance as the basis for their dissatisfaction (Mason & Goulden, 2006). In view of the likely connection between a woman's dissatisfaction with the doctoral program and her thinking about leaving the program, we considered it important to understand in detail her experience of work/career and family/life conflict issues.

The primary areas of career-life concerns expressed by the women we interviewed fell mainly into three clusters that we label lack of family support and understanding, struggles with the biological clock, and difficulty with juggling multiple roles. We discuss here the experiences described by the women Ph.D. students in the physical sciences, mathematics, and engineering with respect to the career and life conflict clusters we identified.

Lack of Family Support and Understanding

Most people desire to have their lives viewed as having meaning and value and to have their decisions respected. However, women who believe they must choose between having a family or a career are reminded every day of the dichotomous choice that faces them—if not today, then tomorrow. Although it is difficult to resist the bombardment of messages in the media about what constitutes an appropriate life for a woman, the modeling and expectations communicated by family members and significant others are perhaps more compelling. The influence of parents, siblings, and other family members on educational attainment and women's careers has been well documented. In the humanities, Nettles and Millett (2006) reported that fully 34 percent of their participating humanities doctoral students had at least one parent who held a Ph.D. or first professional degree. Furthermore, in their study of Ph.D. students in engineering, 39 percent of the parents of women doctoral students had achieved a doctoral or first professional degree, compared to 21 percent of the parents of male doctoral students (Nettles & Millett, 2006).

An international student describes the pressure she gets from her parents to make getting married the top priority:

> I worked hard for three years, collected enough money, and then came here. I went through hell for that. And then I worked here, and then I got my master's here. It took me a year off to decide whether I wanted to do a PhD, but that was primarily because my parents were like, "It's high time you need to get married." For a year, it was like I was in a state of limbo, not knowing where I am going. And so then I said, "To hell with everything. I'm not getting married; I'm doing a PhD."

More than a few women gave poignant testimony about how families of origin transmit the potent gender role expectations for women. One woman constructs her situation as a zero sum game and has difficulty identifying whether her parents do or do not support the choices she has made to pursue a Ph.D.:

> I'm the oldest in my family to not be married. I mean they know that this is what makes me happy, but they definitely would prefer if I had a more traditional . . . at least the other portion of my life. To be honest, I think they're very happy that this is my career, but they don't like the fact that it comes as a zero, it has to be a zero sum game. I don't have time to have children. I don't have. I gave up getting married so that I could get a PhD. So, I don't think they understand how important this is to me. I'm aware of what I've given up to be able to do this.

Struggles with the Biological Clock: If Not Now, Then When?

The ages when women have the highest probability of beginning families and having healthy pregnancies and healthy babies overlap with the typical years during which academic women are in doctoral programs, take postdoctoral positions, begin their academic careers, and endure the stresses of building their research programs and portfolios for tenure. For example, in the natural and social sciences, the mean ages of starting and completing a Ph.D. program are 23 and 32, respectively, and the mean ages from starting a tenure-track position to being awarded tenure are 34 to 39 or later (NSF, Survey of Earned Doctorates, 1999).

Recent data indicate that more men than women doctoral students (but nonetheless a large proportion of women) have spouses or partners (68 percent of men, 59 percent of women in education; 57 percent of men and 51 percent of women in the humanities) except in the sciences and mathematics where more women (53 percent) than men (49 percent) had spouses or partners (Nettles & Millett, 2006). Among women who desire to have children via pregnancy and are racing against the biological clock, not being in a committed relationship poses additional hurdles. More than four of every ten women in doctoral programs are unmarried during their doctoral studies.

Women in committed relationships increasingly weigh their options as their biological window begins to close. One 31-year-old woman in our focus groups described how she shaped her academic plans around family formation: "I just got married last year. I want to graduate by the time I'm 33 so that I can have a child." The struggle of a married Mexican-American doctoral student was apparent as she described her worries about the present and the future:

> I've gotten to the point where I'm thinking, "Why am I doing this PhD?" I'd love to have a family. I'd love to have kids. I went to my OB/GYN exam, and the nurse said to me, "Do you know you have to have kids before you're 35?" Sometimes I just think I should start having children. What if I'm too old? To have a piece of paper and to say, "I picked the paper before kids." Some men I meet think I made that choice. I didn't make that choice. I can't help making that choice. For me it's hard because people will generally say, "Oh, she decided not

to have a family." I've already started thinking what if my ovaries stop working? Should I freeze my eggs, and you hear about early menopause.

We're in that age where every one of our friends is having children. Everyone is like, "Aren't you going to have children soon?" I'm going to turn 28 this year. And in Mexico, that's a huge thing. Not having children before 30—that's really weird. I think that in spite of his being Mexican, he's being really supportive of that. What's going to happen after the PhD? I'm thinking I may be daydreaming thinking everything is going to change.

Although many want and intend to have children, Ph.D. students in most fields appear to be foregoing pregnancies during the predoctoral years. Nettles and Millett (2006) reported that over 80 percent of the doctoral students in the sciences and mathematics, humanities, engineering, and the social sciences reported having no dependent children, compared to about half of the education students. There are gender differences, with fewer women than men reporting they have children under the age of eighteen (Nettles & Millett, 2006).

Further, it is significant to note that about one in four women in Ph.D. programs across all institution types has dependent children, but the variations are large when one examines the type of university as classified by the Carnegie Foundation or the Advancement of Teaching. Women doctoral students with dependent children (41 percent of women versus 34 percent of men) are more likely to be found at research-intensive universities rather than at research-extensive (top-tier) universities where only 20 percent of women doctoral students and 23 percent of men have dependent children (data derived from the National Center for Educational Statistics and NPSAS, 2004). Although many factors likely contribute to these differences, the numbers appear to corroborate the notion that combining doctoral programs and mothering is the most difficult in the most competitive universities. The findings from Mason and Goulden (2006) that 42 percent of women Ph.D. students in the University of California (UC) system (versus 16 percent of men) cite "issues related to children" as the reason for shifting their career goal away from "Professor with Research Emphasis" reinforce the conception that graduate student women alter their educational and career paths when they have or anticipate having children.

Women who are pregnant as graduate students often face a host of obstacles. Faculty and peers may be either dismissive or overly solicitous with pregnant women, continuing the long history of perceptions that pregnancy represents a lack of seriousness about academic work or career intentions. Many women are concerned about the negative consequences and loss of privileges that even the disclosure of pregnancy elicits. One of the Ph.D. student men in our focus groups shared that his pregnant wife, also a Ph.D. student in engineering, had in February not yet revealed to her advisor that she was pregnant and set to deliver in May!

Women graduate students who work in disciplines where they may be exposed to toxins, be required to do heavy lifting, or engage in extended trips or demanding field work may need to alter or curtail their activities during the pregnancy. One focus group participant who worked with chemicals was grateful to her advisor who suggested she proceed with her writing and other elements that would not affect her pregnancy:

> If I had a different advisor, I would have had to quit or take time off to have a kid and then it's really hard to come back. So I think the support that you get from an advisor is very important, and that's the only reason I'm still here. Otherwise, I would not be here.

As discouraged as some women may be about forming families while in graduate school, they are at least as worried about the potential for having a family later along with an academic future. The tenure and biological clocks continue to tick in unison. But additionally, women students watch their peers and female faculty and see little hope for improvement and hope for escaping the harsh ways in which women with babies or children are judged. The pervasive double standard only reinforces women's worries: "Young women faculty complain that men with children are seen as leading healthy, balanced lives, while women with children are considered less devoted to their jobs" (Marcus, 2007, p. 29). As the women in our focus groups suggested, the reminders are ubiquitous:

- "I was shocked at Northwestern. A female faculty member got pregnant and a male student said, 'She has no business getting pregnant. She doesn't have tenure.' That is discouraging to me. He will become faculty and hand that idea down."

- "I wonder…it only gets worse later. I think about the expectations of faculty. How the hell will I ever have a baby?"

- "Kids? Nobody wants to hire you if you have a toddler in tow—people say you won't be able to compete or get as much done. Hearing this is discouraging if you want to have kids."

Difficulty with Juggling Multiple Roles

Students who commit themselves to making good progress in their doctoral programs and preparing themselves for the tough competition ahead in landing an academic position do not have much time for anything else in their lives. Doctoral students yearn for more time to socialize, exercise, and have leisure time. In Mason and Goulden's (2006) study, half of the women students who were dissatisfied with their Ph.D. programs felt they did not have enough time for themselves in terms of recreation and health. But when women assume additional roles such as spouse, mother, caretaker, or housekeeper, the amount of stress and guilt they experience may outweigh the pleasures derived from families and clean houses.

In general, being married while in graduate school facilitates persistence, but being married helps men more than women. Married men do better than single men in finishing their Ph.D. degrees in less time, in publishing, and in getting a tenure-track position. Married women finish their programs some-what earlier and have more publications while in graduate school than do single women but are not more likely to get a tenure-track position within the first six months after graduation (Price, 2006).

Other research has indicated that for women who are married to other graduate students, the marriage advantage may be reduced. There is a relatively high number of dual-student couples in graduate school. In the Nettles and Millett (2006) study, almost one-third of the married students had spouses who were also students. In the sciences and mathematics fields, 45 percent of women doctoral students compared to 38 percent of men doctoral students had spouses who were students. When both partners in a couple are pursuing Ph.D. degrees and particularly if they both aim for academic positions, their future career prospects become more challenging and compromises become more likely. It should not be surprising, therefore, that Mason and Goulden (2006) found that about one out of every three women Ph.D. students (compared to one out of five men) cited "issues related to spouse/partner" as the reason for shifting away from a goal of becoming a research professor.

With regard to the experience of women in our focus groups, those who were married or in committed relationships virtually all described the nurturing and sustaining qualities of their partners and how grateful they were to be able to have their support as they proceeded through the doctoral program. The accounts changed, however, when children were part of the picture. Several comments illustrate the additional complications:

- "I have a 2 year old and a husband, and while my husband and family are supportive of my studies, I definitely feel some inadequacies in the three most important roles in my life: mother, wife, student. Most of the time I feel that I'm not giving enough to each of these roles, which makes me feel inadequate in all areas of my life. Sometimes I feel that it's cultural, being Mexican-American, and sometimes I think that it's my age. I'm not quite sure."

- "Actually, when I started my husband quit his job. He said he'd take care of children. It didn't happen. I had to work and pay for the babysitter and find time to do my chores as a PhD student."

- "Actually having kids changes it very, very much. You always think it [having children] can wait, but potentially you could wait forever, so I decided to have a kid. And then you pretty much have to reconsider everything. I think the kids are the biggest difference."

- "I think [having kids] is just part of just what you want as a woman. When I started out, I was just really into it [the Ph.D. program], but then I got married, and I had a kid too. So that was hard, just physically, all the things you have to do. And emotionally too. As a woman, you think differently than a man does. I think it's harder to focus, you know, once you have a family."

These accounts are congruent with the conclusions reached by some that marriage and children may derail women's academic careers. Xie & Shauman

(2003) combined a career trajectory perspective with a detailed statistical analysis of seventeen national data sets to construct "synthetic cohorts" of women. Their findings follow: married women with children are most likely to leave the sciences and engineering after degree completion and are less likely to be employed, get promoted, and be mobile geographically than married men with children or women without children (whether married or not).

Faculty Women

Despite the fact that more women than ever have doctoral degrees, they remain in lower ranks (80 percent of full professors are men), are less likely to be tenured (60 percent of full-time male faculty; 42 percent of full-time female faculty), are more likely to be employed part-time (women represent 36 percent of the full-time faculty and 45 percent of the part-timers), are more often employed at institutions of lesser prestige (women comprise 23 percent of the total full-time faculty at public research universities and 45 percent of the full-time faculty at public two-year colleges), and are under-represented in science and engineering (10 percent of the full professors are women).

As reflected in our previous citations, Mason and Goulden (2002, 2004) at the University of California have collected a great deal of data on the relationship between faculty career advancement and marriage and children for men and women. Their findings substantiate the conclusions reached by other researchers that marriage and families influence the careers of women and that women's careers affect marriages and family life.

Pursuit of Academic Careers Affects Decisions about Marriage and Commitment

Sonnert and Holton (1995) found that more women (34.6 percent) than men (27.3 percent) reported that career demands influenced their decision not to marry. Women who are awarded tenure are more than twice as likely as tenured faculty men to be single twelve years after earning a doctoral degree. Women who are married when they start faculty positions are much more likely than men who are married to divorce or separate from their spouses (Mason & Goulden, 2006).

A Partner's Work or Career May Influence Where, How, and in What Position Academic Women Work

Married women with Ph.D.s are twice as likely as men to have a spouse who works full time. Only one out of ten women, compared to one out of four men, has a spouse who does not work.

Women Scientists with Ph.D.s Are Far More Likely Than Men Scientists to be Married to Another Scientist

In physics, for example, 68 percent of women physicists were found to be married to male scientists, while only 17 percent of male physicists were married to female scientists (MacNeil & Sher, 1999). Dual-career couples inevitably face challenges with regard to locating satisfying and stable positions within a common geographical area (Gilbert, 1993). The "two body" problem is exacerbated when both are academics and there are few colleges and universities in an area, and it is acute when both partners are in the same academic field. The conflicts around these issues may lead to career or relationship compromises (Preston, 2004) and may account for the larger proportions of women in part-time and non-tenure-track positions and at two-year and less prestigious institutions.

Women's Academic Careers Affect Family Formation

Mason and Goulden (2004) analyzed the NSF/National Institutes of Health Survey of Earned Doctorates that follows 160,000 Ph.D. recipients across all fields longitudinally to age 76. They found that the answer to the issue of whether academic careers among women affects their having children depends on whether a woman takes a "fast-track" (top-tier research university) position or a "second-tier" (adjunct, part-time, temporary, or not working) one. Two out of three faculty women in research-extensive universities do not become mothers. Among science and humanities faculty, 44 percent of women are married with children, compared to 70 percent of the faculty men. Where women have taken second-tier positions, there is no difference between men and women in regard to having children or marital stability. Although these findings can be partially explained by differences in the goals and values of women who enter different fields, it is also reasonable to hypothesize that women with children opt for the less pressured and pressuring institutions as a strategy for embracing both of their valued career and family goals.

In contrast, only one in three women who takes a position in a research university before having a child ever becomes a mother and over 50 percent of tenured women in such institutions have never had a child in the household—whether a biological child, a stepchild, or a foster child. Career trumping children appears to be a deliberate decision in many cases: Among married faculty who decided not to have children, three out of four women cited career considerations compared to fewer than half of the men (Sonnert & Holton, 1995). However, society has a powerful "motherhood mandate" (Russo, 1976) that stigmatizes women who do not want to have children, so social desirability may affect women's attributions for their decisions. It is very difficult for a woman to say that she was never all that interested in having a child, while a demanding career and being committed to science are respected reasons for avoiding childbearing.

Family Formation Affects Faculty Women's Academic Careers

The analysis of survey data in the UC studies led the authors (Mason, Goulden, & Wolfinger, 2004) to the following conclusion: "The message is clear: for women, babies and marriage, particularly in combination, dramatically decrease their likelihood of entering a tenure-track position." Referring to the Berkeley studies, one Radcliffe fellow put it this way: "Motherhood, it turns out, is the killer—what academic women have long suspected has now been demonstrated. Motherhood radically lowers a woman's chance of getting tenure, while it significantly increases a man's." Instead, many Ph.D. moms slip into not-quite-faculty positions (adjunct, part-time, lecturers). In the case of scientists and engineers employed part time, almost eight times as many women (n = 709,200) than men (n = 54,100) cite family responsibilities as the reason they are not working full time (NSF, 2007, Table H-11, p. 247). Similarly, among unemployed people in science and engineering, 27 percent of the women point to family responsibilities as the reason for not working compared to less than 2 percent of the men. (NSF, 2007). Although social desirability in the context of the motherhood mandate might be influencing some responses in these studies, it is clear that for women who do wish to have children, options are limited.

In a qualitative study of faculty women in the sciences and engineering at Georgia Institute of Technology, Fox and Colatrella (2006) found that practically all women agreed that personal factors, including gender and getting along with male colleagues, matter in advancement. The authors also found, however, that the women believed that it is risky to even talk about one's own personal situation, lest it affect her advancement. As one faculty member explained, "It comes at a price. If a person reveals she is pregnant, for example, some people will think that makes more work for them....It is risky to open [one's] mouth and be classified as a troublemaker" (Fox & Colatrella, 2006, p. 383).

As Brown, Swinyard, and Ogle (2003) observed in their study of academic medicine, "the demands of career and personal life [are] each great enough to extract compromise from the other, and, further, that anticipated support from a partner, the community, and medical center was inadequate to make it possible to success in multiple roles at once" (p. 1005). The relationship between parenting and academic careers for women is reciprocal. Preston's (2004) research revealed that mothers who take a larger role with child care cut back on the nonessentials like having lunch with colleagues, doing overtime, traveling to conferences, and outside reading. All these activities are important contributors to career advancement. Similarly, Mason and colleagues (Mason, Stacy, Goulden, Hoffman, & Frasch, 2005) found that among thousands of faculty parents in the University of California system, the majority report that they had found it necessary to slow down their careers as a result of their parenting roles. However, being a parent still affects women's careers more: two out of three faculty mothers reported slowing down for parenting compared to half of the faculty fathers.

Timing Matters When It Comes to Babies

Mason and Goulden (2004) compared the academic careers of women and men who had babies within five years after their Ph.D.s ("early babies") and the academic careers of women and men who had babies after five years past the Ph.D. They found that women Ph.D.s with early babies were 38 percent less likely than men with early babies to achieve tenure. Women with "late babies" were as likely to achieve tenure as women without children.

Stress and the Academic Way

We all get just twenty-four hours in a day. But for women starting out in the academy, finding time to fit in priorities may be even tougher. According to a recent NSF study (Hoffer & Grigorian, 2005) among Ph.D.-level scientists and engineers, those who work in higher education work more hours per week on average than those in industry jobs and government workers. Tenure-track faculty who had not yet received tenure reported the longest workweeks on average.

In a University of California survey of 4,400 tenure-track faculty, women with children and in the age category of thirty to fifty are the busiest, reporting over 100 hours per week in professional, care giving, and household responsibilities, compared to men with children and in the same age group who report spending eighty-five hours on these responsibilities (Mason, et al., 2005). It is sobering to note what has changed since the 1980s when similar studies were conducted. In one survey of 651 employees of a Boston-based corporation (presumably with more clearly defined work hours than Mason, et al.'s faculty), married mothers averaged eighty-five hours occupied with work, child care, and home care, compared to married fathers who averaged sixty-six hours (cf. Hochschild, 1989). In twenty years, then, the "leisure gap" between women and men has narrowed by four hours, but each parent has fifteen to nineteen hours less time available per week! A simple calculation reveals that if Mason's faculty women sleep eight hours per night, they are left with an average of one hour and forty minutes per day to choose among exercise, spending time with partners or friends, leisure reading, or other worthy pursuits.

The academic life, which requires travel time away from home and the intellectually intensive activities of writing and publishing, raises the level of energy needed just for that role alone. It is not surprising that work and family stress is pervasive for faculty parents, as one woman responded to Handelsman and colleagues (2005):

> I feel like my career is a constant gamble to strike the right balance between three things: (i) how much I must commit myself to my career in order to get tenured/ remain a competitive scientist/earn enough clinical revenue; (ii) how much time and effort I give to my husband/ household to stay married; and (iii) how much time and effort I give to my children to guide their growth and development.

Of course, academics are not alone in juggling roles. According to a 2003 survey conducted by Widmeyer Research and Polling of Washington, D.C., more than eight out of ten Americans wish they had more time to spend with their family and six out of ten reported that they felt pressured to work too much (Center for the New American Dream, 2003). It is interesting, however, that almost one in three said they would be willing to trade a pay cut for more time. University faculty, especially the early career women, do not have that option if they wish to achieve tenure.

On Regrets and Missed Opportunities

Commitments to work and family are widely considered to be the primary tasks of healthy adult development (Erickson, 1968; Levinson, 1978; Vaillant, 1977), although most early developmental scholars studied only men. Even if women do not desire to have children, they have social bonds with other family members. While career and vocational psychologists have come to recognize that social connections are an essential function of work for all people (e.g., Blustein, 2006), the central role of social connection and relationships in women's lives has received substantial attention (Cross & Madsen, 1997). Some feminists (e.g., Gilligan, 1982; Miller, 1976) have argued that women define competence as interdependence, that is, in terms of their affiliations and close connections with others compared to male conceptions of competence that are based on autonomy and instrumentality.

It is important to remember, too, that women are by no means a homogeneous group with uniform aspirations and that unique histories and contexts may affect developmental processes that in turn may create psychologically different cohorts (Stewart & Ostrove, 1998). For example, different commitments and life patterns can be expected from women with an interpersonal orientation than from those with personality domains characterized by instrumentality and assertiveness or valuation of social norms (Vandewater & Stewart, 1998).

For both men and women, however, fulfilling aspirations and reaching goals have long been recognized as related to psychological health and wellness. Conversely, people who report regrets about missed opportunities and lifestyle patterns score lower in life satisfaction (Torges, Stewart, & Miner-Rubino, 2005). What complicates the picture of linking motivations and intentions to behaviors and psychological outcomes is the reality that many people find themselves facing or perceiving competing aspirations or conflicts of commitment. The notion of regrets may be best understood in the context of trade-offs and compensating outcomes (Torges, et al., 2005).

Not much is known about the alternatives women select when they leave before finishing doctoral programs, leave tenure-track or tenured positions, or choose to take positions outside of the academy. For many women, selecting an alternative to completing a degree or launching or sustaining an academic career may be a healthy response to their situations and contexts. For example, talented women may choose to pursue MBA degrees where they can earn their degrees in two predictable years and where the *average* starting salary last year was over $92,000, the signing bonus was close to $18,000, and the most competitive total compensation offers were as high as $169,000 (Bloomberg News, 2007). Other women may choose to take industry or government positions where working hours may be more manageable (Hoffer & Grigorian, 2005), potential for salary growth higher, and career paths more secure.

An important issue deserving study is whether the many women with graduate degrees who opt out of professional careers or make career sacrifices or, alternatively, who sacrifice marriage or commitment and having children to strengthen their career success later regret the choices they made. There are hints in the literature but no careful studies of the particular group of women we target in this chapter. For example, in a pilot study on the regrets and priorities of women, the most frequently cited regrets were related to missed educational opportunities and a perceived lack of assertiveness and the most frequently cited priority was family (Metha, Kinnier, & McWhirter, 1989). Hewlett (2002) found in a survey of high-achieving career women that some regretted not having children despite their success and that certain careers with more flexibility like law and entrepreneurship lent themselves to a better work/family balance. Such research requires special sensitivity given the social script that makes it difficult for women to identify anything other than family as a priority and the taboo on expressing regrets with regard to having had children.

Role quality matters more than the number of roles a woman holds (Vandewater, Ostrove, & Stewart, 1997). Indeed, working is often a matter of financial necessity, regardless of whether a woman has children or not. In 2003, over 78 percent of mothers with children under age eighteen and over 62 percent of mothers with children under age six were in the workforce (Bureau of Labor Statistics, 2004). In longitudinal studies of women educated at Radcliffe and the University of Michigan, women's family role quality, measured in ratings of satisfaction with whatever family or household situation they were in (regardless of whether she had a partner and/or children) in their 40s, was related to concurrent measures of both life satisfaction and psychological well-being. Work role quality (measured as satisfaction with their current work situation) was an important predictor of well-being for the Radcliffe sample, and less important for the Michigan women. For the women who had received bachelor's degrees from Radcliffe, almost half had earned a doctoral degree by age 48 (compared to 24 percent at Michigan), half were pursuing careers as opposed to jobs (compared to 37 percent at Michigan), and 36 percent were "major professionals" (e.g., college professors or physicians), compared to 21 percent at Michigan. The greater frequency of professional careers among the Radcliffe alumni may explain the difference: The authors speculate that work role quality may be more critical for women who pursue careers than for those who work in jobs. The socioeconomic differences between the two groups of women should also be taken into account when interpreting the results.

Mason and Goulden (2004) found that 38 percent of female faculty in the University of California indicated that they had had fewer children than they wanted compared to 18 percent of faculty men. As the authors write, "While not exactly a 'smoking gun,' this report suggests that the tradeoff successful women make between careers and children is not without regret for many."

One difficulty with reaching conclusions based on survey results is that studies are usually done with elite scientists (Grant, et al., 2000) who have managed some type of accommodation to make possible professional and personal roles in one life. It is possible that the scientists who faced the most severe difficulties with juggling roles are no longer participating in a science setting where these surveys reach them. Furthermore, as Grant and colleagues (2000) point out,

> What are obliterated by narrowly focused survey studies are the sacrifices in personal life that women scientists make to do scientific work, or the extraordinary management work they do to coordinate the demands of two greedy institutions that do not blend well with each other....Most endured considerable costs, in terms of sleep loss, near complete loss of leisure time, and stressful days to make it work successfully. (p. 81)

Institutional Approaches: Family-Friendly Models, Use, and Impact

In response to the growing evidence that inflexible academic structures contribute to the difficulty parents experience in integrating career and family lives, many universities have introduced policies and benefit packages to ease the burden. Most of the new initiatives pertain to more flexible arrangements for pregnancy and child care responsibilities among faculty. Only a handful of universities, beginning with MIT and then Stanford, introduced accommodations for graduate students. Stanford's policy, for example, allows pregnant women graduate students the right to a twelve-week period in which they are excused from normal duties to take care of late-stage pregnancy, delivery, and newborn care. During the time granted, students retain their official status and financial support, and they automatically receive a one-term extension on academic requirements (Jaschik, 2005b).

While the initiatives have largely been fueled by the concern over the continued attrition of women from the academic pathways, it is important to note that more may be at stake than just the numbers of women in the professoriate. The late Chief Justice William Rehnquist (2003) referred to the social stakes in a 2003 case as follows:

> Stereotypes about women's domestic roles are reinforced by parallel stereotypes presuming a lack of domestic responsibilities for men. Because employers continued to regard the family as the woman's domain, they often denied them similar accommodations or discourages them from taking leave. These mutually reinforcing stereotypes created a self-fulfilling cycle of discrimination that forced women to continue to assume the role of primary family caregiver, and fostered employers' stereotypical views about women's commitment to work and their value as employee.

The National Science Foundation ADVANCE program has been a catalyst in fostering institutional changes to make it possible and more desirable for academic women to succeed and advance in their university careers. Since the inception of the program in 2001, there have been twenty-eight Institutional Transformation projects funded through the ADVANCE program, and another round of new awards will be made this year. Although the ADVANCE program was designed to increase the number of women scientists and engineers in higher ranks and academic leadership roles, the structural and policy changes that have been implemented at ADVANCE institutions have benefited academic women in general and in many cases, men as well. Importantly, the many presentations and publications that have resulted from the work of ADVANCE leaders and the growing corpus of research and evaluation studies of these interventions have informed efforts at many other institutions.

Based on idiosyncratic and local needs, ADVANCE institutions have designed programs and tested solutions around a number of principal areas faced by women who are combining academic careers and families. New policies have been developed and processes and structures changed to address the constraining tenure clock and dual-career couples and to provide family and pregnancy leave, on-campus child care, and full benefits for non-tenure-track positions. With regard to reducing the conflict between the biological and tenure clocks, universities have crafted more flexible leave policies, allowed for active status with modified duties, and agreed to stop or extend the tenure clock during the years of family formation.

Several institutions have also recognized that an important step is to transfer more control from the administration to the individual so that women and men can better arrange their lives to suit their own needs. Toward this end, several institutions have developed a menu of benefit choices that provide flexibility across the professional life-span. These menus include, for example, selection of work hours, benefits, telecommuting, professional development accounts, financial assistance with child care or eldercare, and assessment and advice about services that are available off campus.

Despite the creation of new policies, there is evidence that many academic women decline to take advantage of them. In one study of respondents from

256 institutions, 24 percent cited fear of reprisal for taking advantage of work/family policies (Sullivan, Hollenshead, & Smith, 2004). Drago, et al. (2006) has called women's efforts to forestall being viewed as needing assistance "bias-avoidance behavior."

As one response to the reluctance of women to accept accommodations for fear of being disadvantaged professionally, a 2005 report from the University of California (Mason, et al., 2005) recommended several major system-wide policy and program recommendations. These included clarifying that UC's existing Active Service-Modified Duties and tenure clock extensions are *entitlements* for faculty with substantial responsibility for the care of a newborn or a newly placed child under age 5 and creating a university-sponsored emergency backup child care system.

The American Council on Education, Office of Women in Higher Education (2005) offered several proposals to institutions that would go beyond what has already been adopted. These include the following:

- Creating tenure-track reentry opportunities for Ph.D.s who stepped out to manage family responsibilities.
- Eliminating hiring penalties for "documented dependent care-related resume gaps."
- Allowing tenure-track or tenured faculty to choose part-time positions that can be used "for a specified period (up to five years) as personal needs arise."
- Creating guidelines for faculty to take multiple-year leaves for personal or professional reasons.
- Offering flexible time frames for probationary periods of up to ten years with reviews at set intervals.

Bold ideas are needed, and individuals as well as organizations and academic institutions may be their source. For example, in Germany, Christiane Nüsslein-Volhard, a famous women geneticist who shared the 1995 Nobel Prize in medicine for her work on early embryonic development, established an unusual grant program that supports female scientists with children. The grants, drawn from a foundation established with her Nobel Prize money, pay for housekeeping. The money is intended not only to offset the cost of duties that women commonly assume, even if they are scientists, but also to help women resist the societal pressure to make a tidy home a woman's priority.

Mobilizing Support for Change

Challenging the socially accepted male norms about how academic work is defined, accomplished, and rewarded may change the conditions under which women have labored in universities (Blackburn & Lawrence, 1995). Indeed, most women agree that what they need is a wife. But as Hochschild wrote almost twenty years ago when as a new assistant professor she was bringing her infant son to her office hours in Barrows Hall on the UC Berkeley campus, "maybe they don't need 'wives'; maybe they need careers basically redesigned to suit workers who also care for families. This redesign would be nothing short of a revolution, first in the home, and then at places of work" (Hochschild, 1989, p. x).

While some women in earlier cohorts may have been willing to make professional or personal sacrifices in the face of their preparation for academic careers, it may be the case that young academics today, both women and men, will demand an environment that allows for a satisfying home life. The search for well-being by today's aspiring academics may be quite different than what is considered a good life by Baby Boomer women (Goldin, 2004). In fact, because young faculty men today make career sacrifices for parenting and care giving at a much higher rate than senior male faculty (Mason, Stacy, & Goulden, 2003), faculty men may be strong allies in urging universities to accommodate their partners' and their own search for a more balanced life. As one researcher put it, "It's time for a 'national dialogue' on how colleges can make faculty jobs more attractive to those who want 'a life of the mind and the heart'" (Jaschik, 2005).

If universities wish to remain competitive for attracting and retaining top faculty, and as both men and women continue to forge new arrangements for balancing academic careers and satisfying family lives, new patterns will have to evolve beginning with how faculty peers and administrators interact with faculty who are parents. Mary-Claire King, a geneticist at the University of California at Berkeley and member of the National Academy of Sciences who has five patents and 200 articles, offers this perspective:

> By far the biggest obstacle is how to have enough hours in the day to be the mother of a young child and do the work. You cannot do everything well. You cannot control how experiments will work and how many times you'll have to do them. And there's nothing about raising a young child that you can control. There are no easy solutions to that....I think it is impossible to drop out [of science] and drop back in. I think one needs to stay in, which means that lab directors need to be patient with people who need to leave at 4:30 and go pick up at day care. (Wilson, 2005)

Challenging the Metrics

As long as the current academic structures and reward systems in research universities are sustained, the academy will remain largely incompatible with achieving the quality of life and the balance of career and family that faculty, especially faculty women, desire. As universities continue to operate in the academic milieu of rankings and ratings, they will engage in fierce competition to recruit the most Nobel Laureates, National Academy, and endowed chairs, and they will seek to shape faculty activities toward increased external funding and high volumes of publications in prestigious journals and publishing houses.

As institutions continue to ramp up their expectations for faculty and for students in order to strengthen their competitive advantage along traditional metrics, there will continue to be less room and less success for people who do not fit that mold. The participating doctoral candidates and recent Ph.D.s in one study (Moyer, Salovey & Casey-Cannon, 1999) bemoaned that they are constantly battling the underlying assumption that one cannot be a good research scholar and faculty member unless she or he makes an exclusive commitment to devote all energy and time to work in a competitive and frenetic environment that in actuality is antithetical to the nurturing of creativity and innovation.

What if the metrics for evaluating faculty performance were replaced or at least broadened to include, for example, the following?

- Assigning priority to a critical mass of seminal publications over a lengthy list of inconsequential ones;
- Giving more weight to student learning, impact of mentoring students, and student placements and career paths than to the number of students in a class or the number of memberships on student committees;
- Encouraging creative alternatives to instructional schedules and modalities that enhance learning for nontraditional students;
- Providing opportunities to barter assignments and cooperative child care.

Conclusion

Women continue to experience both progress and challenges in their struggle for gender equity in the academy. Although change has been steady, progress has been slow. Women, and even more so ethnic minority women, are still lagging far behind men in the tenure-track, tenured, full rank, and leadership positions of American universities and colleges. The gap is even larger in the first-tier universities that aspire to recruit and retain world-class scholars. When one broadens the concept of gender equity to include not only career outcomes but also family outcomes, the inequities become even more pronounced.

Career-family conflict issues continue to be major barriers to women's participation in science, technology, engineering, and mathematics (STEM) careers. Failure to provide effective means for integrating academic work and family responsibilities continues to have severe and long-lasting effects on academic women's lives.

Graduate school is a formative period in which female graduate students solidify their views on their ability to lead a balanced and integrated life. These views shape career choices, with each choice determining later options. Academic, institutional, and cultural changes are necessary to enhance the ability of women faculty to incorporate both careers and families in their lives and to achieve greater balance among their various roles. Such changes have an impact beyond their effects on the faculty women who are participating in them. These women serve as the role models and mentors of future generations of STEM women who are observing the difficulties faced by faculty women and making inferences about their own futures based on what they see. Further, broadening the scope of family-friendly policies to encompass support for graduate women, even if they only observe their peers and do not personally take advantage of them, sends the message that their life choices are valued and that it is possible to achieve a fulfilled and balanced life and still pursue a career in their chosen field.

So we still have considerable work to do if we are to meet the goal articulated in the AAUP's 2001 *Statement of Principles on Family Responsibilities and Academic Work*: "to create an academic community in which all members are treated equitably, families are supported, and family-care concerns are regarded as legitimate and important."

In the words of the late Denise Denton, a strong voice for women in STEM fields:

> The current situation is untenable and unacceptable. We must unite to ensure that all of our nation's people are welcomed and encouraged to excel in science and engineering at our colleges and universities.
> Our nation's future depends on it. (2005, p. 27)

Acknowledgment and Disclaimer

This material is based upon work supported by the National Science Foundation under Grant No. 0634519.

Any opinions, findings, and conclusions or recommendations expressed in this material are those of the author(s) and do not necessarily reflect the views of the National Science Foundation.

Note

This research is supported by a grant to Bianca L. Bernstein from the National Research Foundation Research and Evaluation on Education in Science and Engineering (REESE) program, NSF/REC #0634519.

References

American Association of University Professors (2006). *AAUP faculty gender equity indicators 2006.*

American Council on Education (ACE), Office of Women in Higher Education (2005). *An agenda for excellence: Creating flexibility in tenure-track faculty careers.* Washington, DC: American Council on Education. http://www.acenet.edu/bookstore/pdf/2005_tenure_flex_summary.pdf.

Anderson-Rowland, M., Bernstein, B.L., & Russo, N.F. (2007). The doctoral program experience in engineering and computer science: Is it the same for women and men? *Proceedings of the WEPAN 2007 Conference*, WEPAN—Women in Engineering Programs and Advocates Network.

Bailyn, L. (2003). Academic careers and gender equity: Lessons learned from MIT. *Gender, work and organizations, 10*(2), 137–153.

Banaji, M.R., & Greenwald, A.G. (1995). Implicit stereotyping and prejudice. In M.P. Zanna & J.M. Olson (Eds.). *The psychology of prejudice: The Ontario Symposium* (Vol. 7, pp. 55–76). Hillsdale, NJ: Lawrence Erlbaum.

Bandura, A. (1986). *Social foundations of thought and action: A social cognitive theory.* Englewood Cliffs, NJ: Prentice Hall.

Bandura, A. (1997). *Self-efficacy: The exercise of control.* New York: Freeman.

Berg, H.M., & Ferber, M.A. (1983). Men and women graduate students: Who succeeds and why? *Journal of Higher Education, 54*(6), 629–648.

Bernstein, B.L., Horan, J., & Anderson-Rowland, M. (2006). *CareerBound: Internet-delivered resilience training to increase the persistence of women PhD students in STEM fields.* NSF-REC 0634519. Arlington, VA: National Science Foundation.

Bernstein, B.L., Russo, N.F., & Anderson-Rowland, M. (2007). Everyday encouragers and supports for women in STEM PhD programs. In B.L. Bernstein (2007). Symposium on predictors of science and engineering involvement: Three NSF-funded studies. San Francisco: American Psychological Association.

Blackburn, R.T., & Lawrence, J.H. (1995). *Faculty at work: Motivation, expectation, satisfaction.* Baltimore, MD: The Johns Hopkins University Press.

Bloomberg News (2007). New MBAs awash in offers: Heavy recruiting sends pay soaring. *Baltimore Sun,* March 15, 2007. http://www.baltimoresun.com/business/bal-bz.mba15mar15,0,897879.story?coll=bal-business-headlines.

Blustein, D.L. (2006). *The psychology of working: A new perspective for career development, counseling, and public policy.* Mahwah, NJ: Lawrence Erlbaum.

Bronstein, P., Rothblum, E.D., & Solomon, S. (1993). Ivy halls and glass walls: Barriers to academic careers for women and ethnic minorities. In R. Boice & J. Gainen (1993). *New directions for teaching and learning, No. 53.* San Francisco: Jossey-Bass.

Brown, A.J., Swinyard, W., & Ogle, J. (2003). Women in academic medicine: A report of focus groups and questionnaires, with conjoint analysis. *Journal of Women's Health, 12*(10), 999–1008.

Bureau of Labor Statistics (2007). Employment status of the population by sex, marital status, and presence and age of own children under 18. Washington, DC: U.S. Department of Labor. http://www.bls.gov/news.release/famee.t05.htm.

Center for the New American Dream (2003). Americans eager to take back their time. http://www.newdream.org/live/time/timepoll.php.

Clark, S.M., & Corcoran, M. (1986). Perspectives on the professional socialization of women faculty: A case of accumulative disadvantage. *The Journal of Higher Education, 57*(1), 20–43.

Cole, J.R. (1979). *Fair science: Women in the scientific community.* New York: The Free Press.

Committee on Maximizing the Potential of Women in Academic Science and Engineering & Committee on Science, Engineering, and Public Policy, National Academy of Sciences, National Academy of Engineering, and Institute of Medicine (2006). *Beyond bias and barriers: Fulfilling the potential of women in academic science and engineering.* Washington, DC: National Academies Press.

Committee on Professionals in Science and Technology (CPST, 2006). *Four decades of STEM degrees, 1966–2004: "The devil is in the details."* STEM Workforce Data Project: Report No. 6. Washington, DC: CPST.

Cross, S.E., & Madsen, L. (1997). Models of the self: Self construals and gender. *Psychological Bulletin, 122,* 5–37.

Danecke, D.D. (2005). PhD completion project: Preliminary results from baseline data. *Council of Graduate Schools Communicator, 38*(9), 1–8.

Daniell, E. (2006). *Every other Thursday: Stories and strategies from successful women scientists.* New Haven, CN: Yale University Press.

Denton, D. (2005, Dec. 9). Closing comments. National academy's convocation on biological, social, and organizational components of success, December 9, 2005, Washington, DC. Quoted in Committee on Maximizing the Potential of Women in Academic Science and Engineering & Committee on Science, Engineering, and Public Policy, National Academy of Sciences, National Academy of Engineering, and Institute of Medicine (2006). *Beyond bias and barriers: Fulfilling the potential of women in academic science and engineering.* Washington, DC: National Academies Press, chap. 6, p. 27.

Drago, R., Colbeck, C.L., Stauffer, K.D., Pirretti, A., Burkum, K., Fazioli, J., Lazzaro, G., & Habasevich, T. (2006). The avoidance of bias against caregiving: The case of academic faculty. *American Behavioral Scientist, 49,* 1222–1247.

Erikson, E. (1968). *Identity: Youth and crisis.* New York: Horton.

Etzkowitz, H., Kemelgor, C., & Uzzi, B. (2000). *Athena unbound: The advancement of women in science and technology.* Cambridge: Cambridge University Press.

Fox, M.F., & Colatrella, C. (2006). Participation, performance, and advancement of women in academic science and engineering: What is at issue and why. *Journal of Technology Transfer, 31,* 377–386.

Frasier, H.S. (2006). *PhD Completion Project: Using the baseline data. 2006 CGS*Summer Workshop, Technical Workshop. Washington, DC: Council of Graduate Schools. http://www.cgsnet.org/portals/0/pdf/mtg_sm06Frasier.pdf.

General Accountability Office (2004, July). *Report on women's participation in the sciences.* Washington, DC: U.S. GAO.

Gilbert, L.A. (1993). *Two careers/One family.* Newberry Park, CA: Sage Publications.

Gilligan, C. (1982). *In a different voice: Psychological theory and women's development.* Cambridge, MA: Harvard University Press.

Goldin, C. (2004). Long road to the fast track: Career and family. *Annals of the American Academy of Political and Social Science, 596,* 20–35.

Grant, L., Kennelly, I., & Ward, K.B. (2000). Revisiting the gender, marriage, and parenthood puzzle in scientific careers. *Women's Studies Quarterly, 28,* 62–85.

Hall, R.M., & Sandler, B.R. (1982). Out of the classroom: A chilly campus climate for women? *Project on the Status and Education of Women.* Association of American Colleges: Washington, DC.

Handelsman, J., Cantor, N., Carnes, M., Denton, D., Fine, E., Grosz, B., Hinshaw, V., Marrett, C., Rosser, S., Shalala, D., & Sheridan, J. (2005). More women in science. *Science, 309,* 1190–1191.

Hewlett, S.A. (2002). *Creating a life: Professional women and the quest for children.* New York: Talk Miramax Books.

Hirshman, L.R. (2006). *Get to work: A manifesto for women of the world.* New York: Viking.

Hochschild, A. (1989). *The second shift.* New York: Avon Books.

Hoffer, T.B., & Grigorian, K. (2005). *All in a week's work: Average work weeks of doctoral scientists and engineers.* InfoBrief NSF 06-302, Arlington, VA: National Science Foundation.

Jaschik, S. (2005a). Life of the mind and of the heart. *Inside Higher Ed*, February 2, 2005, http://insidehighered.com/news/2005/02/02/paths.

Jaschik, S. (2005b). New rights for pregnant grad students. *Inside Higher Ed*, Nov. 15, 2005. http://insidehighered.com/news/2005/11/15/stanford.

Keller, E.F. (1996). Feminism in science. In E.F. Keller & H.E. Longino (Eds.). *Feminism and science*. (pp. 1–16). New York: Oxford University Press.

Keller, E.F., & Longino, H. (Eds.) (1996). *Feminism and Science*, New York: Oxford University Press.

Lent, R.W., Brown, S.D., & Hackett, G. (2000). Contextual supports and barriers to career choice: A social cognitive analysis. *Journal of Counseling Psychology*, *47*, 36–49.

Levinson, D.J. (1978). *The seasons of a man's life*. New York: Alfred A. Knopf.

MacNeil, L., & Sher, M. (1999). The dual career couple problem. *Physics Today*, *52*(7), 32–37.

Marcus, J. (2007). Helping academics have families and tenure too: Universities discover their self-interest. *Change*, *39*(2), 27–32.

Mason, M.A., & Goulden, M. (2006). *UC Doctoral Student Career Life Survey*. http://ucfamilyedge.berkeley.edu.

Mason, M., & Goulden, M. (2004). Do babies matter (Part II)? Closing the baby gap. *Academe*, *90*(6), 1–10.

Mason, M., & Goulden, M. (2002). Do babies matter? The effect of family formation on the lifelong careers of academic men and women. *Academe*, *88*(6), 21–23.

Mason, M., Goulden, M., & Wolfinger, N. (2004). Redefining gender equity in the academy. *Annals of the American Academy of Political and Social Science*, *596*, 86–103.

Mason, M., Stacy, A., & Goulden, M. (2003). The UC Faculty Work and Family Survey, 2003. http://ucfamilyedge.berkeley.edu.

Mason, M., Stacy, A., Goulden, M., Hoffman, C., & Frasch, K. (2005). *Faculty family friendly edge: An initiative for tenure-track faculty at the University of California*. Berkeley, CA: University of California.

Metha, A.T., Kinnier, E.H., & McWhirter, E.H. (1989). A pilot study on the regrets and priorities of women. *Psychology of Women Quarterly*, *13*, 167–174.

Miller, J.B. (1976). *Toward a new psychology of women*. Boston: Beacon Press.

Moustakas, C. (1994). *Phenomenological research methods*. Thousand Oaks, CA: Sage.

Moyer, A., Salovey, P., & Casey-Cannon, S. (1999). Challenges facing female doctoral students and recent graduates. *Psychology of Women Quarterly*, *23*, 607–630.

National Center for Educational Statistics (2004). Washington, DC: U.S. Department of Education.

National Postsecondary Student Aid Study (2004). Washington, DC: U.S. Department of Education.

National Research Council, Committee on Women in Science and Engineering (2001). *From scarcity to visibility: Gender differences in the careers of doctoral scientists and engineers*. Washington, DC: NRC.

National Research Council, Committee on Women in Science and Engineering (2001). *Female engineering faculty at U.S. institutions: A data profile*. Available at http://www7.nationalacademies.org/cwse/.

National Science Foundation (1999). *Survey of earned doctorates, 1999–2000*. Arlington, VA: NSF.

National Science Foundation (2004). *Women, minorities, and persons with disabilities in science and engineering: 2004*, NSF 04-317. Arlington, VA: NSF, http://www.nsf.gov/statistics/wmpd/minwomen.htm.

National Science Foundation, Division of Science Resources (2007). *Women, minorities, and persons with disabilities in science and engineering: 2007.* Arlington, VA: NSF.

Nelson, D.J. (2005). A National Analysis of Diversity in Science and Engineering Faculties at Research Universities. Norman, OK: University of Oklahoma. http://cheminfo.chem.ou.edu/~djn/diversity/briefings/Diversity%20Report%20 Final.pdf.

Nerad, M. (1992). Using time, money, and human resources efficiently in the case of women graduate students. *Conference proceedings, Science and Engineering Programs: On Target for Women?* Washington, DC: National Academy of Sciences, National Research Council, Office of Scientific and Engineering Personnel.

Nerad, M., & Cerny, J. (1999). Widening the circle: Another look at women graduate students. *CGS Communicator, 32*(6), 1–7.

Nettles, M.T., & Millett, C.M. (2006). *Three magic letters: Getting to PhD.* Baltimore: The Johns Hopkins University Press.

Nevill, S.C., & Chen, X. (2007). *The path through graduate school: A longitudinal examination 10 years after bachelor's degree.* (NCES 2007-162). U.S. Department of Education. Washington, DC: National Center for Education Statistics.

O'Connell, A.N., & Russo, N.F. (Eds.) (1988). *Models of achievement: Reflections of eminent women in psychology,* Volume II. New York: Lawrence Erlbaum.

O'Connell, A.N., & Russo, N.F. (Eds.) (1983). *Models of achievement: Reflections of eminent women in psychology,* Volume I. New York: Lawrence Erlbaum.

Polkinghorne, D.E. (1989). Phenomenological research methods. In R.S. Valle & S. Halling (Eds.). *Existential-phenomenological perspectives in psychology.* (pp. 41–60). New York: Plenum.

Preston, A.E. (2004). *Leaving science: Occupational exit from science careers.* New York: Russell Sage Foundation.

Price, J. (2006). Does a spouse slow you down? Marriage and graduate school outcomes. http://www.ilr.cornell.edu.ezproxy1.lib.asu.edu/cheri/wp/cheri_wp94.pdf.

Pritchard, P.A. (Ed.) (2006). *Success strategies for women in science: A portable mentor.* San Diego, CA: Elsevier Press.

Rehnquist, W. (2003). Nevada Department of Human Resources et al. v. Hibbs et al. *certiorari* to the United States Court of Appeals for the Ninth Circuit, No. 01-1368. Argued January 15, 2003—Decided May 27, 2003. http://caselaw.lp.findlaw.com/ scripts/printer_friendly.pl?page=us/000/01-1368.html.

Richardson, M.S. (1993). Work in peoples' lives: A location for counseling psychologists. *Journal of Counseling Psychology, 40,* 425–433.

Rosser, S.V. (2004). *The science glass ceiling: Academic women scientists and the struggle to succeed.* New York: Routledge.

Russo, N.F. (1976). The motherhood mandate. *Journal of Social Issues, 32,* 143–154.

Siegel, L. (2005). A study of PhD completion rates at Duke University. *Council of Graduate Schools Communicator, 38*(1), 1–7.

Sonnert, G., & Holton, G. (1995). *Gender differences in science careers.* New Brunswick, NJ: Rutgers University Press.

Stewart, A.J., & Healy, J.M., Jr. (1989). Linking individual development and social changes. *American Psychologist, 44,* 30–42.

Stewart, A.J., & Ostrove, J.M. (1998). Women's personality in middle age: Gender, history, and midcourse corrections. *American Psychologist, 53,* 1385–1394.

Sullivan, B., Hollenshead, C., & Smith, G. (2004). Developing and implementing work-family policies for faculty. *Academe, 90*(6), 24–27.

Torges, C.M., Stewart, A.J., & Miner-Rubino, K. (2005). Personality after the prime of life: Men and women coming to terms with regrets. *Journal of Research in Personality, 39* (10), 148–165.

Vaillant, G.E. (1977). *Adaptation to life.* Cambridge, MA: Harvard University Press.

Valian, V. (1999). *Why so slow: Advancement of women.* Boston, MA: MIT Press.

Valian, V. (2007). Women at the top in science—and elsewhere. In S.J. Ceci, & W.W. Williams (Eds.). *Why aren't more women in science? Top researchers debate the evidence.* Washington, DC: American Psychological Association.

Vandewater, E.A., Ostrove, J.M., & Stewart, A.J. (1997). Predicting women's well-being in midlife: The importance of personality development and social role involvements. *Journal of Personality and Social Psychology, 72,* 1147–1160.

Vandewater, E.A., & Stewart, A.J. (1998). Making commitments, creating lives: Linking women's roles and personality at midlife. *Psychology of Women Quarterly, 22,* 717–738.

Wilson, R. (2004). Where the elite teach, it's still a man's world. The women who do get hired at major research universities often find a "toxic atmosphere." *The Chronicle of Higher Education,* Dec. 3, A9–A14.

Wilson, R. (2005). Women in the National Academy: Four newly honored scientists talk about being selected, their work, and making their mark in research. *Chronicle of Higher Education,* June 10, A1–A10.

Xie, Y., & Shauman, K.A. (2003). *Women in science: Career processes and outcomes.* Cambridge, MA: Harvard University Press.

Zwick, R. (1991). *Differences in graduate school attainment patterns across academic programs and demographic groups.* Princeton, NJ: ETS and GRE Minority Graduate Education Project.

CHAPTER 8

Integrating Work/Life: Resources for Employees, Employers, and Human Resource Specialists

Michele A. Paludi and Carmen A. Paludi, Jr.

The following resources are intended to provide employers and human resource specialists with suggestions for developing policies, procedures, and training programs on topics related to work/family balance. These resources are based in empirical research and the case law cited throughout this book. Policies and training programs have been developed and used by Human Resources Management Solutions (Michele Paludi, President) in its human resource consulting. We recommend that employers adapt these resources to meet their individual needs, taking into account, for example, whether the business is unionized. These policies do not necessarily reflect employment laws of all states in the United States or other countries. We invite you to use the policies and training programs as samples and adapt them to your own organization's culture. We also recommend you have all of your employment policies reviewed by your organization's legal counsel.

Sample Workplace Policies

Family and Medical Leave Policy

The Family and Medical Leave Act (FMLA) is intended to allow employees to balance their work and family life by taking reasonable unpaid leave for a serious health condition, for the birth or adoption of a child, and for the care of a child, partner/spouse provided for by [Name of Company] or parent who has a serious health condition. The Act is intended to balance the demands of the workplace with the needs of families as well as promoting equal employment opportunity for men and women.

[Name of Company] employees are eligible if they have worked for the Company for at least twelve months (not required to be consecutive) and worked at least 1,250 hours in the twelve months preceding the commencement of the leave.

Eligible employees are able to use up to a total of twelve weeks of leave in any fiscal year with proper medical documentation for the following types of absences:

* An employee's own serious health condition;
* The serious health condition of an employee's immediate family member;

"Serious health condition" means an illness, injury, impairment, or physical or mental condition that involves

— Any period of incapacity or treatment connected with inpatient care (i.e., an overnight stay) in a hospital, hospice, or residential medical care facility; or
— A period of incapacity requiring absence of more than three calendar days from work, school, or other regular daily activities that also involves continuing treatment by (or under the supervision of) a health care provider; or
— Any period of incapacity due to pregnancy, or for prenatal care; or
— Any period of incapacity (or treatment therefore) due to a chronic serious health condition (e.g., asthma, diabetes, epilepsy, etc.); or
— A period of incapacity that is permanent or long-term due to a condition for which treatment may not be effective (e.g., Alzheimer's, stroke, terminal diseases, etc.); or,
— Any absences to receive multiple treatments (including any period of recovery therefrom) by, or on referral by, a health care provider for a condition that likely would result in incapacity of more than three consecutive days if left untreated (e.g., chemotherapy, physical therapy, dialysis, etc.).

* Caring for a newborn or newly placed adopted child or foster child

Leave to care for a newborn child or for a newly placed child must conclude within twelve months after the birth or placement.

[Name of Company] may require that the need for leave for a serious health condition of the employee or the employee's immediate family member be supported by a certification issued by a health care provider. [Name of Company] will allow the employee at least fifteen calendar days to obtain the medical certification. Spouses/partners employed by the Company may be limited to a combined total of twelve workweeks of family leave for the following reasons:

* Birth and care of a child;
* For the placement of a child for adoption or foster care, and to care for the newly placed child;
* To care for an employee's parent who has a serious health condition.

During the unpaid leave, employees retain the same medical and dental coverage and must still contribute the same amount toward medical benefits as they paid before the leave began.

The FMLA permits employees to take leave on an intermittent basis or to work a reduced schedule under certain circumstances. Intermittent/reduced schedule leave may be taken when medically necessary to care for a seriously ill family member or because of the employee's serious health condition. Intermittent/reduced schedule leave may be taken to care for a newborn or newly placed adopted or foster care child only with the employer's approval.

Employees needing intermittent/reduced schedule leave for foreseeable medical treatment must work with their employers to schedule the leave so as not to unduly disrupt the employer's operations, subject to the approval of the employee's health care provider. In such cases, the employer may transfer the employee temporarily to an alternative job. An employee returning to work following an FMLA leave may be able to

> (1) return to the same job with the same rights, benefits, pay and other terms and conditions which existed prior to the leave or (2) return to an equivalent position with equivalent rights, benefits, pay and other terms and conditions of employment.

Any benefits, seniority, etc., in place immediately before the leave will be reinstated provided that the employee returns to work the first work day following the end date of the FMLA leave or any approved leave up to thirty days following the FMLA leave.

While on unpaid leave, an employee will not accrue seniority or service time for eligibility for a performance review, salary review, adjustment, or bonus.

Employees should contact _____ should they wish to take FMLA. They will

— Provide to the employee requesting information the FMLA documentation within two business days of a request;
— Maintain appropriate documentation to support or deny a leave request;
— Require the employee to use concurrently with the FMLA leave the following paid leaves in the order listed:

> Sick leave available for use, as defined by the contract, rule, or policy governing the reason for the leave, followed by

> Vacation leave in excess of ten days, to which the employee is entitled.

Employees will be required to contact _____ at least every four weeks to report on their status and intention to return to work at the end of their leave.

HIV/AIDS Nondiscrimination Policy

[Name of Company] does not unlawfully discriminate against applicants or employees living with or affected by the Human Immunodeficiency Virus (HIV) or Acquired Immune Deficiency Syndrome (AIDS).

HIV is a blood-borne virus and is spread only through intimate contact with blood, semen, vaginal secretions, and breast milk. Scientists continue to make new discoveries about HIV infection and AIDS. But one piece of information has never changed—how the disease spreads. Scientists have recognized this fact since 1982. The basic facts about HIV transmission and prevention are sound.

[Name of Company] is committed to maintaining a safe and healthy learning and work environment for all employees. This commitment stands on the recognition that HIV, and therefore AIDS, is not transmitted through any casual contact.

[Name of Company] recognizes that HIV infection and AIDS, the most serious stage of disease progression resulting from HIV infection, pose significant and delicate issues for the Company. Accordingly, [Name of Company] has established the following guidelines and principles to serve as the basis for dealing with employee situations and concerns related to HIV infection and AIDS.

[Name of Company] will treat HIV infection and AIDS the same as other illnesses in terms of all of its employee policies. Employees living with or affected by HIV infection and AIDS will be treated with compassion and understanding, as would employees with other disabling conditions.

In accordance with the law, [Name of Company] will provide reasonable accommodations for employees and applicants with disabilities who are qualified to perform the essential functions of their positions. This applies to employees and applicants living with HIV infection and AIDS and is especially relevant in light of new treatments for HIV infection that may allow people living with AIDS to return to work after periods of disability leave.

Generally, disabled employees have the responsibility to request an accommodation. It is [Name of Company's] policy to respond to the changing health status of employees by making reasonable accommodations. Employees may continue to work as long as they are able to perform their duties safely and in accordance with performance standards.

Employees are asked to contact _____ for assistance in making reasonable accommodations.

Recognizing the need for all employees to be accurately informed about HIV infection and AIDS, [Name of Company] will make information and educational materials available. Individuals who want to obtain information and materials should contact _____.

Employees are expected to continue working relationships with any employee who has HIV infection or AIDS. Individuals who refuse to work with, withhold services from, harass, or otherwise discriminate against an employee with HIV infection or AIDS will be subject to the same disciplinary procedures that apply to other [Name of Company] policy violations.

Information about an employee's medical condition is private and must be treated in a confidential manner. In most cases, only administrators directly involved in providing a reasonable accommodation or arranging benefits may need to know an employee's diagnosis. Others who may acquire such information, even if obtained personally from the individual, should respect the confidentiality of the medical information.

Information on HIV testing and other AIDS services is available from your supervisor.

If you have questions about this policy, its interpretation, or the information upon which it is based, please contact your supervisor.

Policy on Domestic Violence as a Workplace Concern

Employees of [Name of Company] must be able to work in an atmosphere of mutual respect and trust. As a place of work, [Name of Company] should be free of violence and all forms of intimidation and exploitation. [Name of Company] is concerned and committed to our employees' safety and health. The Company refuses to tolerate violence in our workplace.

[Name of Company] has issued a policy prohibiting violence in the workplace. We have a zero tolerance for workplace violence.

[Name of Company] also will make every effort to prevent violent acts in this workplace perpetrated by spouses, mates, or lovers. The Company is committed to dealing with domestic violence as a workplace issue. [Name of Company] has a zero tolerance for domestic violence.

Domestic Violence: Definition

Domestic violence—also referred to as battering, spouse abuse, spousal assault, and intimate partner abuse—is a global health problem. This victimization is defined as violence between adults who are intimates, regardless of their marital status, living arrangements, or sexual orientations. Such violence includes throwing, shoving, and slapping as well as beatings, forced sex, threats with a deadly weapon, and homicide.

Domestic Violence: Myths and Realities

Myth: Domestic violence affects a small percentage of employees.
Reality: Approximately 5 million employees are battered each year in the United States. Domestic violence is the leading cause of injury and workplace death to women in the United States.
Myth: People must enjoy the battering since they rarely leave the abusive relationship.

Reality: Very often victims of battering do leave the relationships. Women and men remain in a battering relationship not because they are masochistic, but for several well-founded reasons, e.g.,

- Threats to their lives and the lives of their children, especially after they have tried to leave the batterer;
- Fear of not getting custody of their children;
- Financial dependence;
- Feeling of responsibility for keeping the relationship together;
- Lack of support from family and friends;
- The batterer is not always violent;
- They still love the batterer.

Myth: Individuals who batter abuse their partners because they are under a great deal of stress, including being unemployed.
Reality: Stress does not cause individuals to batter their partners. Society condones partner abuse. In addition, individuals who batter learn they can achieve their goals through the use of force without facing consequences.
Myth: Children are not affected by watching their parents in a battering relationship.
Reality: Children are often in the middle of domestic violence. They may be abused by the violent parent. Children may also grow up to repeat the same behavior patterns they witnessed in their parents.
Myth: There are no long-term consequences of battering.
Reality: There are significant long-term consequences of battering, including depression, anger, fear, anxiety, irritability, loss of self-esteem, feelings of humiliation and alienation, and a sense of vulnerability.
Myth: Domestic violence occurs only in poor and minority families.
Reality: Domestic violence occurs among all socioeconomic classes and all racial and ethnic groups.

Threat Assessment Team

[Name of Company] has established a Threat Assessment Team to assist with dealing with workplace violence. Part of the duties of the Threat Assessment Team is to assess the vulnerability of the Company to domestic violence and serve as advocates for victims of workplace violence, including domestic violence that has carried over into the workplace.

Each of these members of the Threat Assessment Team has received specialized training in workplace violence issues, including domestic violence as a workplace concern.

Services Offered by [Name of Company] for Employees Who Are Victims of Domestic Violence

[Name of Company] will offer the following services for our employees who are victims of domestic violence:

- Provide receptionists and building security officer with a photograph of the batterer and a description of the batterer;
- Screen employee's calls;
- Screen employee's visitors;
- Accompany the employee to her or his car;
- Permit the employee to park close to the office building;
- When there is a restraining order, the Vice President will send a formal notification to the batterer that indicates that his or her presence on the Company premises will result in arrest;
- Referrals for individual counseling.

Threat Assessment Team Members

[Insert names and titles]

Policy Statement on Sexual Harassment

[Name of Company] has an obligation to create a work environment for all employees that is fair, humane, and responsible—an environment that supports, nurtures, and rewards career progress on the basis of such relevant factors as work performance.

All employees of [Name of Company] have a responsibility to cooperate in creating a climate at [Name of Company] where sexual harassment does not occur. We have a zero tolerance for sexual harassment of our employees. All employees at all levels of [Name of Company] must not engage in sexual harassment.

The following policy statement is designed to help employees of [Name of Company] become aware of behavior that is sexual harassment and the procedures [Name of Company] will use to deal with sexual harassment in a way that protects complainants, witnesses, and respondents.

What Is Sexual Harassment?

Sexual harassment is legally defined as "unwelcome sexual advances, requests for sexual favors, and other verbal or physical conduct of a sexual nature" when any one of the following criteria is met:

Submission to such conduct is made either explicitly or implicitly a term or
condition of the individual's employment;

Submission to or rejection of such conduct by an individual is used as the basis for
employment decisions affecting the individual;

Such conduct has the purpose or effect of unreasonably interfering with an
individual's work performance or creating an intimidating, hostile, or offensive
work environment.

There are two types of sexual harassment situations that are described by
this legal definition: quid pro quo sexual harassment and hostile environment
sexual harassment.

Quid pro quo sexual harassment involves an individual with organizational
power who either expressly or implicitly ties an employment decision to
the response of an employee to unwelcome sexual advances. Thus, a supervisor may promise a reward to an employee for complying with sexual requests (e.g., a better job, promotion, or raise) or threaten an employee's job
for failing to comply with the sexual requests (e.g., threatening to not promote the employee or threatening to give an unsatisfactory performance
appraisal).

Hostile environment sexual harassment involves a situation where an
atmosphere or climate is created in the workplace that makes it difficult, if
not impossible, for an employee to work because the atmosphere is perceived
by the employee to be intimidating, offensive, and hostile.

For purposes of this policy, sexual harassment includes, but is not limited
to, the following:

— Unwelcome sexual advances;
— Sexual innuendos, comments, and sexual remarks;
— Suggestive, obscene, or insulting sounds;
— Implied or expressed threat of reprisal for refusal to comply with a sexual
  request;
— Patting, pinching, or brushing up against another's body;
— Sexually suggestive objects, books, magazines, poster, photographs, cartoons,
  e-mail, or pictures displayed in the work area;
— Actual denial of a job-related benefit for refusal to comply with sexual
  requests.

Thus, sexual harassment can be physical, verbal, visual, or written. These
behaviors constitute sexual harassment if they are committed by individuals
who are in supervisory positions or co-workers. And these behaviors constitute sexual harassment if they occur between individuals of the same sex or
between individuals of the opposite sex. [Name of Company] prohibits these
and other forms of sexual harassment. Any employee who engages in such
behavior will be subject to disciplinary procedures.

What Is Not Sexual Harassment?

Sexual harassment does not refer to relationships between responsible, consenting adults. Sexual harassment does not mean flirting. Giving compliments does not mean sexual harassment. Sexual harassment refers to unwanted, unwelcome behavior. Not every joke or touch or comment is sexual harassment. The key is to determine if the behavior is unwanted and unwelcome. Furthermore, sexual harassment interferes with an employee's ability to get her or his work done.

Costs of Sexual Harassment

There are high costs of sexual harassment to individuals. They include depression, feelings of helplessness, headaches, anxiety, sleep disturbances, and disordered eating. The cost of sexual harassment to our company includes decreased productivity, absenteeism, and decreased morale.

What Should Individuals Do If They Believe They Are Being Sexually Harassed?

Employees who have complaints of sexual harassment, including any supervisor, co-worker, vendor, client, or visitor, are urged to report such conduct to [Name of Investigator] so that (s)he may investigate and resolve the problem. Employees are encouraged to bring their concerns to [Name of Investigator] within sixty days of the alleged incident(s). Employees may ask [Name of Investigator] to postpone an investigation if the performance appraisal of the employee will be performed by the party against whom the complaint is brought.

[Name of Investigator] will investigate all complaints as expeditiously as possible in a professional manner. The confidentiality of the investigative procedures will be maintained. The complaint will be investigated and resolved typically within a two-week period.

Complainants and those against whom complaints have been filed will not be expected to meet together to discuss the resolution of the complaint.

Investigatory procedures have been developed and are fully explained in another memorandum: [Name of Company] Sexual Harassment Complaint Procedure.

Any employee who is found to have engaged in sexual harassment will be subject to disciplinary action, as indicated in [Name of Company] complaint procedure.

Discussions about Sexual Harassment: No Complaints

Employees at [Name of Company] have the right to seek advice and information about sexual harassment from [Name of Investigator], who will maintain such consultation in confidence. Such discussions do not constitute filing a complaint of sexual harassment.

Retaliation

There will be no retaliation against employees for reporting sexual harassment or assisting [Name of Investigator] in the investigation of a complaint. Any retaliation against such individuals is subject to disciplinary action, including verbal and written reprimands, transfers, demotions, and dismissal.

False Complaints

If after investigating any complaint of sexual harassment it is discovered that the complaint is not bona fide or that an individual has provided false information regarding the complaint, that individual may be subject to disciplinary action, including verbal and written reprimands, transfers, demotions, and dismissal.

Recommended Corrective Action

The purpose of any recommended corrective action to resolve a complaint will be to correct or remedy the injury, if any, to the complainant and to prevent further harassment. Recommended action may include a private or public apology, written or oral reprimand of the individual who engaged in sexual harassment, relief from specific duties, suspension, transfer, or dismissal of the individual who engaged in sexual harassment.

If complainants are not satisfied with the attempts to resolve the sexual harassment, they may seek resolution through other sources, for example, the [Name of State] Division of Human Rights or the Equal Employment Opportunity Commission.

Policy Review

This policy will be reviewed periodically by [Name of Investigator] and by [Name of President], who welcome comments on the policy, its interpretation, or implementation.

For additional information regarding sexual harassment, contact [Name of Investigator] or [Name of President]. They have been trained in complaint resolution and receive additional education about sexual harassment law and its management and psychological applications. Both [Name of Investigator] and [Name of President] will be responsible for a program of information and education concerning this policy and procedures relating to sexual harassment.

Office Numbers and Phone Numbers

[Insert numbers]

Complaint Procedures

Employees of [Name of Company] who have complaints of sexual harassment by anyone at this Company, including any supervisors, are encouraged to report such conduct to [Name of Investigator] so that (s)he may investigate and resolve the problem. Individuals who feel subjected to sexual harassment should report the circumstances orally and/or in writing within sixty days to [Name of Investigator].

[Name of Investigator] will maintain confidentiality in her or his investigation of complaints of sexual harassment.

Any employee pursuing a complaint may do so without fear of reprisal.

Informal Advice and Consultation

Employees may seek informal assistance or advice from [Name of Investigator]. All such consultations will be confidential, and no action involving any individual beyond [Name of Investigator] and the employee will be taken until a formal complaint has been made.

[Name of Investigator] may, however, take action, within the context of existing policy and procedures, that (s)he deems appropriate on the basis of information received to protect all employees of [Name of Company].

Resolutions of Informal Complaints

Any employee may discuss an informal complaint with [Name of Investigator]. If the employee who discusses an informal complaint is not willing to be identified to the person against whom the informal complaint is made, [Name of Investigator] will make a confidential record of the circumstances and will provide guidance about various ways to resolve the problem.

If the employee bringing the complaint is willing to be identified to the person against whom the complaint is made and wishes to attempt an informal resolution of the problem, [Name of Investigator] will make a confidential record of the circumstances (signed by the complainant) and undertake appropriate discussions with the person complained about.

When a number of people report incidents of sexual harassment that have occurred in a public context (for example, offensive sexual remarks in an office setting) or when [Name of Investigator] receives repeated complaints from different employees that an individual has engaged in sexual harassment, the person complained against will be informed without revealing the identity of the complainants.

Resolutions of Formal Complaints

If an employee wishes to pursue the matter through a formal resolution, a written complaint must be submitted to [Name of Investigator], giving details of the alleged harassment, including dates, times, places, name(s) of individual(s) involved, and names of any witnesses.

The complaint must be addressed to [Name of Investigator].

Formal complaints will be investigated in the following manner:

Upon receipt of a written complaint, [Name of Investigator] will immediately forward a copy of the complaint, along with a copy of [Name of

Company] Sexual Harassment Policy Statement and Procedures, to the individual complained against and request a meeting within three days.

The investigation will be limited to what is necessary to resolve the complaint or make a recommendation. If it appears necessary for [Name of Investigator] to speak to any individuals other than those involved in the complaint, (s)he will do so only after informing the complainant and person complained against.

[Name of Investigator] will investigate all complaints of sexual harassment expeditiously and professionally. To the extent possible, the investigation will be completed within two weeks from the time the formal investigation is initiated.

[Name of Investigator] will also maintain the information provided to her or him in the complaint and investigation process confidential. The only other employee of [Name of Company] who will be informed about the investigation is [Name of President], President of [Name of Company].

[Name of Company]'s first priority will be to attempt to resolve the complaint through a mutual agreement of the complainant and the person complained against.

If an employee making a formal complaint asks not to be identified until a later date (e.g., until the completion of a performance appraisal), [Name of Investigator] will decide whether or not to hold the complaint without further action until the date requested.

If a formal complaint has been preceded by an informal investigation, [Name of Investigator] shall decide whether there are sufficient grounds to warrant a formal investigation.

The names or other identifying information regarding witnesses for either party involved in the complaint will not be made known to the opposing party.

Referrals for therapists and medical personnel for all individuals involved in an investigation will be made available upon request.

Following the completion of an investigation, [Name of Investigator] will make one of the following determinations:

— Sustain the Complaint: A finding of sexual harassment has been made and recommendations for corrective action will be identified. Recommended corrective action may include an apology, written or oral reprimand, relief from specific duties, suspension, dismissal, or transfer of the employee found to have engaged in sexual harassment.
— Not Sustain the Complaint: A finding of no sexual harassment has been made.
— Insufficient Information: Insufficient information exists on which to make a determination. [Name of Investigator] will reinvestigate all parties named in the complaint.

Following any determination and recommendations for corrective action, [Name of Investigator] will issue a written decision with findings of fact and reason to [Name of President]. [Name of President] will correspond with the complainant and person complained against of the findings of the investigation and recommendations for corrective action. Appropriate statements of apology will be made to employees involved in the complaint by [Name of President].

If complainants are not satisfied with the attempts to resolve their complaint of sexual harassment, they may seek resolution through other sources, for example, the [Name of State] Division of Human Rights or the Equal Employment Opportunity Commission.

For additional information regarding [Name of Company] zero tolerance of sexual harassment, contact

Name of Investigator
  Office Number
  Phone Number
Name of President
  Office Number
  Phone Number

Both [Name of Investigator] and [Name of President] are trained in complaint resolution and receive additional education about sexual harassment law and its management and psychological applications.

In addition, [Name of President] and [Name of Investigator] will be responsible for a program of information and education concerning sexual harassment in general and [Name of Company] policy and procedures.

Disability Nondiscrimination Policy

[Name of Company] does not discriminate on the basis of disability in the recruitment, hiring, and retention of employees.

Defining "Disability"

An individual with a disability is defined by law as someone who

- Has a physical or mental impairment that substantially limits one or more major life activities,
- Has a record of having such an impairment, or
- Is regarded as having such an impairment.

Learning disabilities is a general term that refers to a heterogeneous group of disorders manifested by significant difficulties in the acquisition and use of listening, speaking, reading, writing, reasoning, or mathematical abilities. These disorders are intrinsic to the individual, presumed to be due to central nervous system dysfunction and may occur across the life span.

Reasonable Accommodation

[Name of Company] will make an accommodation to the known disability of a qualified applicant or employee if it would not impose an "undue hardship" on the Company. Undue hardship is defined by law as an action requiring significant difficulty or expense when considered in light of factors such as size, financial resources, and the nature and the structure of its operation.

Reasonable accommodation may include, but is not limited to

- Making existing facilities used by employees readily accessible to and usable by employees with disabilities;
- Acquiring or modifying equipment and/or devices, adjusting training materials, and policies, including providing qualified readers or interpreters.

A modification or adjustment is "reasonable" by law if it "seems reasonable on its face, i.e., ordinarily or in the run of cases." Thus, the request is reasonable if it appears to be plausible or feasible. A reasonable accommodation enables an applicant with a disability to have an equal opportunity to participate in the application process and to be considered for hire in the Company. In addition, a reasonable accommodation permits an employee with a disability an equal opportunity to enjoy the benefits and privileges of employment that employees without disabilities enjoy.

Requesting a Reasonable Accommodation

An individual with a disability must request a reasonable accommodation when she or he knows that there is a barrier that is preventing her or him, due to a disability, from effectively performing her or his duties. [Name of Company] recommends that an individual request a reasonable accommodation before her or his performance suffers or conduct problems occur.

[Name of Company] requests that employees with a physical disability, psychiatric disability, or learning disability provide professional verification by a licensed health care provider who is qualified to diagnosis the disability. This verification must reflect the employees' present level of functioning of their major life activity affected by the disability. The verification must also provide detailed data that support the requests for any reasonable accommodation.

Applicants or employees must pay the cost of obtaining the professional verification. The Company has the discretion to require supplemental assessment of a disability. The cost of the supplemental assessment shall be borne by the employee or applicant. If the Company requires an additional assessment for purposes of obtaining a second professional opinion, then the Company shall bear any cost not covered by any third party.

Employees who are recuperating from temporary injuries or illnesses may request interventions during this stage of recovery. Verification of the temporary impairment must be obtained by employees. The cost of obtaining the professional verification shall be borne by the employee.

An applicant or employee must request a reasonable accommodation by contacting _____ at any time. Written notification of the decision will be mailed to the employee or applicant. The decision can be appealed within ten days by submitting a written request to _____. This decision will be communicated to the individual. There will be no further appeal.

[Name of Company] will not coerce, intimidate, threaten, harass, or interfere with any individual exercising or enjoying her or his rights under the Americans with Disabilities Act or because that individual aided or encouraged another employee in the exercise of rights granted or protected by this Act.

Someone other than the individual with a disability may request a reasonable accommodation on behalf of the individual. Thus, a family member, friend, health professional, or other representative may request a reasonable accommodation on behalf of an applicant or employee.

Requests for reasonable accommodation do not need to be in writing.

All requests for reasonable accommodation will be dealt with expeditiously by [Name of Company].

Applicants and employees may be asked about their ability to perform specific functions. [Name of Company] will not ask applicants or employees about the existence, nature, or severity of a disability.

For additional information, contact your supervisor.

General Time Off Policies

Funeral Leave

In case of death in the immediate family, [Name of Company] will provide up to three days with pay. The immediate family includes parents, mates, children, grandparents, siblings, or other relative for whom you are directly responsible. Additional unpaid time off may also be granted.

Jury Duty

Employees of [Name of Company] who are called to serve on a jury will not lose any wages as a result of performing this legal and civic duty. Employees will receive regular base wages less pay received by them for jury duty to compensate for any actual loss in pay for the period. Employees are expected to report to work on any day or portion of a day that they are excused from jury duty.

Military Leave

Employees of [Name of Company] who are required by law to fulfill a military commitment for a two-week period or less during each summer shall receive their regular base wages during this period less any pay received by them for military service.

Sick Leave

Full-time employees of [Name of Company] with one full year of service will receive two sick days for the calendar year or sixty-four accrued hours after one year of service. For part-time employees, it is thirty accrued hours after one year of service.

Voting

Employees are allowed up to two hours with pay to vote if they do not have two hours continuous off-duty time while the polls are open.

Religious Observances

[Name of Company] makes every reasonable effort to accommodate employees' religious observances. Supervisors may grant time off with pay to employees to observe religious obligations that take place during normal working hours. The lost time must be made up within the same pay period or charged to vacation if available.

Personal Business

Supervisors may grant employees reasonable time off with pay for nonmedical professional appointments or other personal business that cannot be arranged during nonworking hours. The lost time must be made up within the same pay period. If the time is not made up, the absence will be charged to accrued vacation.

Nondiscrimination Policy

[Name of Company] is committed to maintaining a working environment that supports equal rights for all employees. Employment decisions will be based only on merit, performance, and legitimate professional criteria. [Name of Company] prohibits discrimination on the basis of race, sex, religion, age, color, creed, national origin, disability, or sexual orientation, and discrimination against disabled and Vietnam era veterans, in the recruitment or treatment of employees, and in the operation of its activities and programs, as specified by Federal and State Laws.

Application to [Name of Company]

With respect to recruitment, recruitment sources will be advised in writing of [Name of Company] policy and commitment to equal opportunity and must acknowledge their compliance with the program. Applicants are considered with regard to their skills, education, performance, and other bona fide qualifications. Nonmeritorious factors, such as age, race, color, religion, sex, national origin, ancestry, veteran status, sexual orientation, or the presence of a disability may not be considered.

Right to Redress

All employees have the right to redress possible injustices or wrongs done to them. Employees who believe they have been discriminated against may file an oral and/or written complaint with _____ [Investigator], stating the nature of the perceived discrimination, the alleged perpetrator, witnesses, and the recommended remedy needed to correct the situation.

Investigation of Complaints

Complaints will be investigated in the following manner:

1. Upon receipt of a written complaint, the Investigator will ask the individual if he or she has any witnesses he or she would like to be interviewed on his or her behalf. Individuals will complete a form providing names of witnesses as well as the issues to which the witnesses may address. Complainants will provide a signed statement giving permission to contact these witnesses.

2. The Investigator will immediately forward a copy of the complaint, along with a copy of [Name of Company] discrimination Policy Statement and Procedures, to the individual complained against and request a meeting with this individual within three business days.

3. During the meeting with the respondent, the Investigator will ask the individual if he or she has any witnesses he or she would like to be interviewed on his or her behalf. Individuals will complete a form providing names of witnesses as well as the issues to which the witnesses may address. Complainants will provide a signed statement giving permission to contact these witnesses.

4. Names or other identifying features of witnesses on behalf of the complainant and respondent will not be made known to the opposing party. This will help ensure participation by witnesses in the investigation.

5. All complaints of discrimination will be investigated expeditiously and professionally. To the maximum extent possible, the investigation will be completed within two weeks from the time the formal investigation is initiated.

   All information provided during the investigation will be treated in a confidential manner. Parties to the complaint will be asked to sign a "Confidentiality" form in which they state they will keep the complaint and complaint resolution confidential. They will also be asked to sign a form indicating they will Not Retaliate against any party to the complaint.

6. A safe environment will be set up for the complainant, the respondent, and the witnesses to discuss their perspectives without the fear of being ridiculed or judged.

7. No conclusions about the veracity of the complaint will be made until the investigation is completed.

8. All documents presented by the parties to the complaint will be reviewed. Documents include, but are not limited to, letters and notes.

9. Following the completion of an investigation, one of the following determinations will be made:

   • Sustain the Complaint: A finding of discrimination has been made and recommendations for corrective action will be identified, including reprimands, relief from specific duties, transfer, or dismissal.

   • Not Sustain the Complaint: A finding of no discrimination has been made.

   • Insufficient Information: Insufficient information exists on which to make a determination. All parties will be reinvestigated.

10. Following any determination and recommendations for corrective action, the Investigator will issue a written decision with findings to _____. _____ will correspond with the complainant and person complained against of the findings of the investigation and recommendations for corrective action. _____ will make appropriate statements of apology to individuals involved in the complaint.

11. If complainants are not satisfied with this procedure, they may seek redress through other sources, for example, the Equal Employment Opportunity Commission.

Any party to a complaint resolution may do so without fear of reprisal.

[Name of Company]'s first priority will be to attempt to resolve the complaint through a mutual agreement of the complainant and the person against whom the complaint was made.

Each complaint against the same individual will be handled independently. Similarly, knowledge that the complainant has filed complaints against other individuals in the past will not enter into the investigative process. Such information may be taken into account in determining sanctions for violation of the nondiscrimination policy.

Referrals for therapists and medical personnel for all individuals involved in an investigation will be made available upon request.

Policy Review

[Name of Company] will review this policy on Equal Opportunity annually in order to ensure its completeness and accuracy in light of changing legislation and conditions.

Training

_____ will be responsible for facilitating training programs for all administrators and employees on this Equal Opportunity Policy.

Time Off/Career Break Policy

[Name of Company] supports the retention of valued staff. [Name of Company] demonstrates our commitment to long-term career development and family commitments by offering a Time Off/Career Break Policy.

The purpose of this Time Off/Career Break Policy is to allow employees an opportunity to leave their employment on a long-term basis (1–5 years), mainly to fulfill family commitments and responsibilities. Employees will be kept up-to-date during their time off and will be assisted in returning to work at the end of the break.

Definition and Purpose of Time Off or Career Break

A time off or career break is a special leave without pay for a specified period of time. The time off or career break is designed for employees who are currently prevented from remaining in full- or part-time work but who would like to restart work when circumstances make this possible, e.g., following raising an infant or having cared for a sick dependent relative. Time off/career breaks may not be allowed for the purpose of taking alternative employment.

Eligibility

To be eligible for time off/career break, employees must have at least two years' service with [Name of Company]. Some examples of where an application for time off/career break may apply are in the context of the following:

Caring for a dependent relative who is ill or disabled;

Taking advanced courses to benefit [Name of Company];

Child care.

Human Resources will consider each application on the merits of the employee's case. A decision will be made within five working days following receipt of the application. Full details will be provided in writing to the employee if his or her application is rejected. The employee may appeal in writing to the President of [Name of Company] within ten working days of being informed of the refusal.

The time off/career break policy does not affect other arrangements for granting unpaid leave.

Duration of Leave

The maximum period for time off/career break is five years. An employee may take a number of breaks throughout his or her employment provided the total periods of absence do not exceed five years. A new application must be made to Human Resources for each time off requested.

Application Process

Applications for time off or career break must be made in writing at least two months prior to the commencement of the proposed break. It is a condition of [Name of Company] that no more than one in every ten members of staff is on a time off/career break at any one time.

All application materials are available from Human Resources.

Employee Responsibilities

Employees who are in time off/career break are obligated to advise Human Resources of any change in circumstances. Employees must be available for at least ten days each year should they be required to attend training, work, etc. If the time off/career break lasts longer than one year, employees must notify Human Resources of their intention to continue the time off at least two months prior to the end of the year.

[Name of Company]'s Responsibilities

[Name of Company] is committed to ensuring that upon returning from a time off/career break, employees will be offered priority consideration for any position at the same salary and rank prior to the break. [Name of Company] will guarantee employees on time off/career break with ten days paid employment per year in order to keep the employee informed about policy changes and procedures and developments in the Company. To ease the transition back to work, employees may be allowed to work on a part-time basis for three months before returning to full-time responsibilities. Employees on time off/career break will not be entitled to sick pay or maternity leave pay.

Telecommuting Policy

Definition

Telecommuting is a work arrangement in which an employee works from a remote work site away from the primary workplace or from home for a portion of the workday or workweek or pay period. Employees may send work to and communicate with the main office via telephone, computer, or fax.

Eligibility

Telecommuting is available to any employee of [Name of Company] who has worked in his or her present position for at least one year. Employees who are currently working in other flexible scheduling arrangements are also eligible for a telecommuting arrangement.

Employees' requests for a telecommuting arrangement must be approved by the Human Resources Department, in collaboration with the employees' immediate supervisor and department head. They will make a decision within five working days following receipt of the application. Full details will be provided in writing to the employee if his or her application is rejected. The employee may appeal in writing to the President of [Name of Company] within ten working days of being informed of the refusal.

Telecommuting Arrangement

The number of days an employee of [Name of Company] may telecommute is left up to the employee in conjunction with the employee's supervisor. It is [Name of Company]'s policy to allow one or two days per week.

Employees of [Name of Company] who have a telecommuting arrangement may not conduct business meetings in their homes. If a meeting is scheduled on a telecommuting day, employees must use the workplace facilities or arrange for teleconferencing.

Should an employee of [Name of Company] be injured while telecommuting, the employee must follow established procedures for on-the-job injuries.

Any telecommuting arrangement made will be on a trial basis for the first three months. This arrangement may be discontinued, at will, at any time at the request of the employee or [Name of Company].

[Name of Company] will determine, with information supplied by the employee and the supervisor, the appropriate equipment needs (including hardware, software, modems, phone and data lines, facsimile equipment, and photocopiers) for each employee working from a telecommuting arrangement. Both the Human Resource and Information System departments will serve as resources in this matter. Equipment supplied by the organization will be maintained by the organization. Equipment supplied by the employee, if deemed appropriate by the organization, will be maintained by the employee. Equipment supplied by the organization is to be used for business purposes only. Each employee on a telecommuting agreement will sign an inventory of all office property and agrees to take appropriate action to protect the items from damage or theft. Upon termination of employment all company property will be returned to the company.

Compressed Workweek Policy

In order to assist employees with meeting child care, eldercare, or other family responsibilities, [Name of Company] provides compressed workweek arrangements. A compressed workweek allows full-time employees of [Name of Company] to work longer days for part of the week or pay period, in exchange for shorter days, or one day off each week or pay period. For example, employees may work four ten-hour days each week, with one day off each week.

[Name of Company] will permit employees to work part time on a temporary or permanent basis. For example, an employee would be permitted to work half-time during the summer months and return to work full time in the fall.

Employees' requests for a compressed workweek arrangement must be approved by the Human Resources Department, in collaboration with the employees' immediate supervisor and department head. They will make a decision within five working days following receipt of the application. Full details will be provided in writing to the employee if his or her application is rejected. The employee may appeal in writing to the President of [Name of Company] within ten working days of being informed of the decision.

Sample Strategies Employers Can Use to Help Employees Integrate Work and Life

- Develop and enforce family-friendly/life-friendly policies.
- Be supportive of job training.
- Be supportive of parent training.
- Offer services for quality child care.
- Offer services for quality eldercare.
- Assist employees in aligning work and school calendars.
- Lessen employee stress.
- Consider on-site child care services.
- Recognize the benefits of combining work and family roles.
- Offer time-based strategies, e.g., telecommuting, flextime, job sharing, compressed workweeks, and part-time work.
- Contract with a local Employees Assistance Program if your company does not have one on site so employees can receive counseling support on a range of issues from financial to legal to family based.
- Contract with a local wellness center if your company does not have one on site to provide programs for employees on health issues, including proper nutrition, exercise, blood pressure monitoring, free mammograms, smoking cessation, and stress management workshops.
- Facilitate training programs on work/life balance for managers.
- Offer time off/career break leaves.
- Offer relocation assistance to employees.

Sample Strategies for Employees Who Need Assistance with Work/Life Integration

- Utilize time management strategies

- — Make daily lists of activities to accomplish
- — Prioritize activities
- — Schedule activities according to the priorities set
- — Deal with the most demanding item on the list during the time when you are most alert

- Increase physical exercise

  - — Aerobics
  - — Walking
  - — Swimming

- Take advantage of options offered by your employer, e.g., flex hours, job sharing, and telecommuting

- Avoid guilt

- Nurture yourself

- Foster a support network of friends and family

- Talk with a therapist or Employees Assistance Program

- Utilize relaxation techniques

  - — Meditation
  - — Hypnosis
  - — Biofeedback

Sample Training Programs

Training Topic: Creating and Managing Family-Friendly Workplace Training for Managers

Goals of Training Program

Discuss the difficulties for employees to balance work and life

Discuss the stressors associated with integrating work and life

Understand the necessity of a flexible workplace

Discuss the organizational challenges that must be met in creating and sustaining a flexible workplace

Discuss strategies to implement successful work/life initiatives

Discuss key management issues that need to be addressed in a flexible workplace

Discuss effective strategies for preventing and managing job stress and burnout

Discuss the role of the Employees Assistance Program in managing a flexible workplace

Understand strategies for implementing family-friendly policies:

Culture Change

Direct Services

Time Based

Money Based

At the Completion of the Training, Managers will be Able to

Understand the necessities for a flexible workplace

Develop family-friendly policies for their workplace

Apply change management tools to overcome barriers to successful work/life programs

Topics for Presentation and Discussion

Welcome and Introductions

Goals of Training

Myths versus Realities about Family-Friendly Policies

Myths

   Employees should keep their personal lives at home

   Face time is more important than productivity

   Management will lose control

   Participation in family-friendly workplaces will be a career-limiting move

Realities

   Flexible policies attracts new employees

   Family-friendly policies retain employees

   Flexible workplaces reduce absenteeism

   Family-friendly workplaces increase production and satisfaction

   Flexible workplaces decrease stress and burnout

Writing and Executing Family-Friendly Policies

Development of Training Programs for Managers and Employees on Family-Friendly Policies

Concluding Comments

Training Topic: Sexual Harassment for Employees

Goals of Training

Define quid pro quo and Hostile Environment Sexual Harassment

Understand Company's Policy Statement and Procedures

Discuss the Interface of Gender and Power in the Workplace

Discuss Psychological Issues Involved in Dealing with Sexual Harassment

Examine the Physical and Emotional Reactions of Being Sexually Harassed

At the Conclusion of this Training, Employees will be able to

Distinguish among Sexual Harassment, Compliments, Flattery, and Flirtation

Identify quid pro quo and Hostile Environment Sexual Harassment

Discuss the Impact of Sexual Harassment on Employees and the Workplace

Discuss Resolution Techniques within the Company

Discuss the Company's Policy and Procedures on Sexual Harassment

Topics for Presentation and Discussion

Introduction to training session and goals of training

What is sexual harassment?

  Legal definition

  Behavioral examples

  Continuum of sexual harassment

  What Constitutes "Workplace setting," including off-work hours at a company-sponsored event

Sexual harassment versus flirtation, compliments, and joking

Hostile environment sexual harassment and gender stereotyping

Impact of sexual harassment on employees

Impact of sexual harassment on workplace

Intent versus impact

Perspective taking

Reporting versus nonreporting: Fear of retaliation

Effective nonverbal communication patterns

Effective verbal communication patterns

Company policy statement and procedures

Resource material for transfer of training

Review and general discussion

Training Topic: Coping with Change
Training for Managers

Goals of Training

Accurately assess employees' problems related to change

Identify appropriate referral resources

Provide appropriate referrals

Provide employees with relevant information about change

Support employees experiencing change

At the Conclusion of the Training Program, Managers will be Able to

Identify the characteristics of personal and organizational change

Understand psychological, physical, behavioral, and organizational consequences
   of dealing with personal and organizational change

Understand strategies for managing transitions and coping with change

Identify interviewing, assessment, and referral strategies for employees
   experiencing changes in either their personal and/or professional lives

Topics for Presentation and Discussion

Welcome, Introductions, and Program Overview

Introductions of Trainers

Introductions of Participants

Review of Agenda

Goals of Training Program

Objectives of Program

What Is Change?

Stages of Change

   Denial

   Resistance

   Exploration

   Commitment

Work/Life Balance and Integration

What Is "Balance?"

When Work/Life Balance Is Disturbed

   Nonwork Factors

      Birth/Adoption of a Child

      Illness

      Death

      New Home

      Eldercare Is Needed

      Deadline

      Discrimination

   Work Factors

      Promotion

      Layoff

      Deadline

      Discrimination

Impact on Children when Work/Family Integration Is Not Achieved

Stress: Coping with Change or Change in Coping?

   Stress Defined

Causes of Stress
  Organizational Factors
    Task demands
      job design, working conditions, physical layout, and work quotas
    Role demands
      role conflicts, role overload, and role ambiguity
    Interpersonal demands
      lack of social support and poor interpersonal relationships
    Organizational structure
      excessive rules and lack of opportunity to participate
    Organizational leadership
      supervisor styles that cause unrealistic pressures, tight controls, and threat of job loss
  Personal Factors
    Family issues
    Personal economic problems
    Trying to balance/integrate work and life roles
Symptoms of Stress
  Emotional Responses
  Physical Responses
  Behavioral Responses
  Organizational Responses
Dealing with "Coping with Change"
Ways Clients Identify Problems
  Directly
  Indirectly
  Substandard Job Performance
Managing the Four Stages of Change
Managing Stress
  Time-Management Techniques
  Physical Exercise
  Relaxation Techniques
  Social Support Network
Managing Others During Change
Concluding Comments

Training Topic: Workplace Stress
Training for Managers

Goals of Training

Identify sources of job stress

Understand impact of job stress on physical and mental health

Identify relationships among job stress, physical health, mental health, and productivity

Ways to change the organization to prevent job stress

At the Conclusion of the Training, Employees will be Able to

Determine what conditions in their organizations may be contributing to employees' job stress

Identify physical and mental health impacts of job stress

Identify the relationship between stress prevention and job performance

Determine ways to change their organization to prevent job stress

Topics for Presentation and Discussion

Welcome and Introductions

Goals of Training

Stress at Work

Scope of Stress in Workplaces

Definition of Job Stress

Contributing Factors to Job Stress

Job Conditions that May Lead to Job Stress

    Managerial Style

    Design of Task

    Interpersonal Relationships

    Work Roles

    Career Concern Issues

Impact of Job Stress on Physical Health

Impact of Job Stress on Mental Health

Stress, Physical Health, Mental Health and Productivity

Warning Signs of Job Stress

Warning Signs of Job Burnout

Dealing with and Preventing Job Stress

    Stress Management

    Organizational Change

Concluding Comments

Topic for Training: Management Styles
Training for Managers

Goals of Training

Identify managerial styles

Understand relationships among managerial style, employee stress, and employee trying to integrate work and family life

Understand what makes an effective manager

Identify common management mistakes

Understand employees juggling multiple roles and responsibilities

At the Conclusion of this Training, Managers will be Able to

Identify their own managerial style

Learn how to integrate other managerial styles in their repertory

Identify ways their learning style is related to employees' stress and job performance

Discuss ways they can change in order to become more effective managers

Identify ways they can be more sensitive to employees who are integrating work and family responsibilities

Topics for Presentation and Discussion

Welcome and Introductions

Goals of Training

Management Styles

Coercive Style
Authoritative Style
Affiliative Style
Democratic Style
Pacesetting Style
Coaching Style

Expanding Repertory of Management Styles

Myths about Managers

Everyone can be a manager
People who get to the top are managers

Managers deliver business results

Managers are great coaches

What Makes an Effective Manager

Ask what needs to be completed

Take responsibility for communication

Ask what is right for the organization

Develop action plans

Take responsibility for decisions

Reframe problems into opportunities

Facilitate productive meetings

Use a "We," not "I," approach to dealing with employees

Common Management Mistakes

Not making the transition from employee to manager

Working for a quick fix instead of a lasting solution

Not setting clear goals

Not delegating responsibilities

Failing to communicate with employees

Not making time for employees

Resisting change

Impact of Managerial Styles on Employees' Stress

Impact of Managerial Styles on Employees Who Need Assistance with Integrating Work and Family

Effective Communication Techniques with Employees

Effective Managing of Employees Who Are Integrating Work and Family Responsibilities

Concluding Comments

Further Reading

Adams, M. (2004). *Change your questions, change your life: 7 powerful tools for life and work*. San Francisco, CA: Berrett-Koehler.

Allen, T. (2001). Family-supportive work environments: The role of organizational perceptions. *Journal of Vocational Behavior, 58*, 414–435.

Archambeau, K., & Archambeau, M. (2006). *Climbing the corporate ladder in high heels.* New York: Career Press.

Barling, J. (Ed.) (2004). *Handbook of work stress.* New York: Sage.

Bond, J., Thompson, C., Galinsky, E., & Protas, D. (2003). *The 2002 national study of the changing workforce.* New York: Families and Work Institute.

Casper, W., Eby, L., Bordeaux, C., & Lockwood, A., & Lambert, D. (2007). A review of research methods in IO/OB work-family research. *Journal of Applied Psychology, 92,* 28–43.

Chick, E. (2004). *Fundamentals of work-life balance.* Alexandria, VA: ASTD Press.

Drago, R. (2007). *Striking a balance: Work, family, life.* New York: Dollars and Sense.

Fine-Davis, M., Fagnani, J., & Giovannini, D. (2006). *Fathers and mothers: Dilemmas of the work-life balance: A comparative study in four European countries.* New York: Springer.

Ford, M., Heinen, B., & Langkamer, K. (2007). Work and family satisfaction and conflict: A meta-analysis of cross-domain relations. *Journal of Applied Psychology, 92,* 57–80.

Friedman, S.D., & Greenhaus, J.H. (2002). *Work and family—Allies or enemies? What happens when business professionals confront life choices.* New York: Oxford University Press.

Gambles, R., Lewis, S., & Rapoport, R. (2006). *The myth of work-life balance: The challenge of our time for men, women and societies.* New York: Wiley.

Golden, T., Veiga, J., & Simsek, Z. (2006). Telecommuting's differential impact on work-family conflict: Is there no place like home? *Journal of Applied Psychology, 91,* 1340–1350.

Grawitch, M.J., Gottschalk, M., & Munz, D.C. (2006). The path to a healthy workplace: A critical review linking healthy workplace practices, employee well-being, and organizational improvements. *Consulting Psychology Journal: Practice and Research, 58,* 129–147.

Halpern, D. (2005). Psychology at the intersection of work and family: Recommendations for employers, working families, and policymakers. *American Psychologist, 60,* 397–409.

Heyman, J. (Ed.) (2000). *The widening gap: Why American working families are in jeopardy and what can be done about it.* New York: Basic Books.

Hill, E., Martinson, V., & Ferris, M. (2004). New-concept part-time employment as a work-family adaptive strategy for women professionals with small children. *Family Relations, 53,* 282–292.

Hill, J., Waldfogel, J., Brooks-Gunn, J., & Han, E.J. (2005). Maternal employment and child development: A fresh look using newer methods. *Developmental Psychology, 41,* 833–850.

Houston, D. (2005). *Work-life balance in the 21st century.* New York: Palgrave Macmillan.

Jackson, M. (2002). *What's happening to home? Balancing work, life and refuge in the Information Age.* Notre Dame, IN: Sorin Books.

Lapierre, L., & Allen, T. (2006). Work-supportive family, family-supportive supervision, use of organizational benefits, and problem-focused coping: Implications for work-family conflict and employee well-being. *Journal of Occupational Health Psychology, 11,* 169–181.

NICHD Early Child Care Research Network (Ed.) (2005). *Child care and child develop-ment: Results from the NICHD Study of early child care and youth development.* New York: Guilford Press.

Schultheiss, D. (2006). The interface of work and family life. *Professional Psychology: Research and Practice, 37,* 334–341.

Somech, A. & Drach-Zahavy, A. (2007). Strategies for coping with work-family con-flict: The distinctive relationship of role ideology. *Journal of Occupational Health Psychology, 12,* 1–19.

Strassel, K., Colgan, C., & Goodman, J. (2006). *Leaving women behind: Modern families, outdated laws.* New York: Rowman & Littlefield Publishers.

Further Reading: Periodicals

Academy of Management Journal
Academy of Management Review
Canadian HR Reporter
Compensation & Benefits Management
Diversity Factor
Focus on Canadian Employment and Equality Rights
HR Magazine
HR Reporter
Human Resource Development International
Human Resource Development Quarterly
Human Resource Management Journal
Human Resource Management Review
Human Resource Planning
Industry Week
International Journal of Human Resource Management
International Journal of Training and Development
Journal of Human Resources
Journal of Organizational Behavior
Journal of Organizational Behavior Management
Journal of Staff Development
Journal of Workplace Learning
MIT Sloan Management Review (formerly Sloan Management Review)
Organizational Behavior and Human Decision Processes
Personnel Psychology
Personnel Review
Training
Training and Development
Training for Quality
Work and Stress

Useful Web Sites for Employees and Employers

All Business Network
   www.all-biz.com
American Bar Association, Commission on Domestic Violence
   http://www.abanet.org/domviol/home.html

American Domestic Violence Crisis Line
  http://www.awoscentral.com
American Psychological Association
  www.apa.org
Business and Professional Women's Organization
  www.bpwusa.org
Center for Leadership and Change Management
  http://leadership.wharton.upenn.edu
Center for Women and Work, Rutgers University
  www.cww.rutgers.edu
Center for Women and Work, University of Massachusetts, Lowell
  www.uml.edu/centers/women-work
Centers for Disease Control and Prevention
  www.cdc.gov
Centre for Families, Work and Well-Being
  www.worklifecanada.ca
Centre for Stress Management
  www.managingstress.com
ElderCare Online
  www.ec-online.net
Elder Focus
  www.elderfocus.com
Employee Assistance Professionals Association
  www.eapassn.org
Families and Work Institute
  www.familiesandwork.org
Feminist Majority Foundation
  www.feminist.org
FindCare Now
  www.findcarenow.com
Harvard Business School Working Knowledge
  www.hbsworkingknowledge.hbs.edu
Inc. Magazine
  www.inc.com
ManagementFirst
  www.managementfirst.com
National Institute for Occupational Safety and Health
  www.cdc.gov/niosh
National Institute of Mental Health
  www.nimh.nih.gov
National Mental Health Association
  www.nmha.org
National Partnership for Women and Families
  www.nationalpartnership.org
Occupational Safety and Health Administration
  www.osha.gov
Office of AIDS Research, National Institute of Health
  www.nih.gov

Office Politics
    www.officepolitics.co.uk/frame.html
Society for Human Resource Management
    www.shrm.org
The Coaching and Mentoring Network
    www.coachingnetwork.org.uk/
The Life Station
    www.thelifestation.com
United States Department of Health and Human Services
    http://www.4women.gov/violence/index.cfm
Virtual-Organization.net
    www.virtual-organization.net
Work and Family Connection
    www.workfamily.com

Index

Page numbers followed by t indicate tables.

About the Editors and Contributors

Editors

MICHELE A. PALUDI, Ph.D., is the author/editor of 26 college textbooks and more than 140 scholarly articles and conference presentations on sexual harassment, psychology of women, gender, and sexual harassment and victimization. Her book *Ivory Power: Sexual Harassment on Campus* (1990, SUNY Press) received the 1992 Myers Center Award for Outstanding Book on Human Rights in the United States. She also was a consultant to and a member of former New York State Governor Mario Cuomo's Task Force on Sexual Harassment. Dr. Paludi serves as an expert witness for court proceedings and administrative hearings on sexual harassment. She has had extensive experience in conducting training programs and investigations of sexual harassment and other EEO issues for businesses and educational institutions. In addition, Dr. Paludi has held faculty positions at Franklin & Marshall College, Kent State University, Hunter College, Union College, and Union Graduate College. She is President of Human Resources Management Solutions.

PRESHA E. NEIDERMEYER, Ph.D., CPA, is an Associate Professor at West Virginia University. She is a consultant with Sphere Capital and is actively involved in sustainable business opportunities in Africa. She has published numerous articles in the area of the effect of culture on auditors and audit behavior.

Contributors

BIANCA L. BERNSTEIN, Ph.D., is a Professor of Counseling Psychology, Educational Leadership & Policy Studies, and Women's Studies at Arizona State University (ASU) in Tempe. She recently completed a term as Director of the Division of Graduate Education at the National Science Foundation, after eight years as Dean of the Graduate College at ASU. Dr. Bernstein specializes in counseling research on stress and cognitive mediation, gender and ethnic issues, and clinical supervision, and in higher education on broadening participation of women and minorities in science and engineering careers, preparing future faculty, and reforming graduate education. Her work has been disseminated through publications in major journals and over 200 presentations at national meetings of scholarly and professional organizations. Dr. Bernstein is the Principal Investigator of a major research grant from the National Science Foundation to improve persistence among women in science and engineering Ph.D. programs.

CRISTINE CIOFFI was educated at Middlebury College and Albany Law School. She is a Past President of the Schenectady County Bar Association. In addition, she is a Trustee of the New York Bar Foundation. She has served as a Schenectady County Legislator. She serves on the Board of Directors of the New York Chapter of National Academy of Elder Law Attorneys.

EROS R. DESOUZA is currently a Professor of Psychology at Illinois State University. He earned his Ph.D. in Community Psychology from the University of Missouri at Kansas City. As a community psychologist, he is deeply interested in social justice. He has carried out qualitative and quantitative research on sexuality and gender issues, including sexual harassment from a cross-cultural perspective. He has written more than 40 scholarly articles, 5 book chapters, and over 90 conference presentations.

KELSEY ALLEN-DICKER earned a B.A. in Psychology at Union College. She graduated in June 2007.

BILLIE DZIECH is a Professor of English at the University of Cincinnati. She coauthored *The Lecherous Professor: Sexual Harassment on Campus* (1984, 1990). In 1989 she published *On Trial: American Courts and Their Treatment of Sexually Abused Children.* This is the first book to examine the experiences of child victims and their families seeking justice in American courts. She has appeared on numerous radio and television shows including *Today, 20/20, The Oprah Winfrey Show,* and *Donahue.* Dziech was the 1994 recipient of the Cohen Award, the University of Cincinnati's highest recognition for Excellence in Teaching. She also received the 1998 Award for Outstanding Scholarly and Professional Activity, also from the University of Cincinnati.

TRACI GRAHAM graduated from Siena College in May 2006 with a B.S. in Marketing Management and a minor in Information Systems. Currently she is pursuing her MBA at Union Graduate College with a concentration in Human Resource Management. Through her education, various internship experiences, and community involvement, Traci hopes to obtain a job in the Human Resource field upon her graduate course work completion in November 2007.

HILARY KASPRZAK lives in Farmington, Connecticut, with her family. She attends Union College in Schenectady, New York, where she is currently majoring in psychology; she plans to graduate in 2008.

JULIE MANNING MAGID is on the faculty at the Kelley School of Business, Indiana University. Her courses focus on law, ethics, and business. Her primary research areas include underdeveloped areas of Title VII and emerging areas of business law.

CARMEN A. PALUDI, JR., brings nearly 26 years of technical and program management experience to human resource management and its related fields. He provides guidance and direction on risk management, and out-of-the-box thought processes for complex systems and scenarios such that policies and procedures developed can be executed. Mr. Paludi is the author of over 20 technical journal articles and numerous presentations to national and international conferences, panels, and technical meetings. He is currently a Senior Scientific Advisor for L-3 Communications, Inc., Engineering Services Group.

NANCY FELIPE RUSSO, Ph.D., is a Regents Professor of Psychology and Women and Gender Studies at Arizona State University. Before that, for nine years she was founder and director of the Women's Programs Office of the American Psychological Association (APA), where she was involved in a variety of research and policy-related activities related to women's health, education, and career development. Author or editor of more than 200 publications related to women and women's issues, Russo is the former editor of *The Psychology of Women Quarterly* and current editor of the *American Journal of Orthopsychiatry*. A Fellow of the American Psychological Association, the American Psychological Society, and the New York Academy of Sciences, Russo has been recognized by APA's Board of Ethnic Minority Affairs for contributions to ethnic minority issues and is the recipient of the American Psychological Association's Award for Distinguished Contributions to Psychology in the Public Interest.

JANET SIGAL received her Ph.D. in Social Psychology at Northwestern University. She is a Professor of Psychology at Fairleigh Dickinson

University. She is a Fellow of Division 35 of the American Psychological Association and a member of the APA UN NGO committee.

MELISSA SMITH graduated from Castleton State College in May 2005 with a Bachelor of Science Degree in Business Administration with a double concentration in Management and Marketing. She currently works for Saint-Gobain Performance Plastics as Human Resource Generalist. She is enrolled in the Certificate of Human Resource Program at The Graduate College of Union University with an expected graduation in the spring of 2008.

REBECCA VACCARIELLO completed a Human Resource Management Certificate at Union Graduate College's School of Management in 2006. She received a J.D. degree from Albany Law School of Union University in 1999. She was an associate attorney at a private law firm with a focus on civil and criminal litigation for six years.

CHRISTA WHITE is currently attending Union College and plans to graduate in June 2008. She is majoring in psychology.